A LOVE NOTE TO
My Tiger Mom

*An Immigrants' daughters' insight to improve
mother-daughter relationship*

JULIA HO

PARTRIDGE
A Penguin Random House Company

To order additional copies of this book, contact
Toll Free 800 101 2657 (Singapore)
Toll Free 1 800 81 7340 (Malaysia)
orders.singapore@partridgepublishing.com
www.partridgepublishing.com/singapore

Contents

About the Author
Julia Ho

Julia has been inspired to write down her heartfelt story of love and how love can be found in different forms of relationships: The relationships between parents and kids, the love between the pairs, and the relationship love of friendships.

The passion of studying love has escalated to another level for Julia, and she went to pursue studies for her Master's of Sexual Health at Sydney University to better understand human nature and people's connections in life.

Through her wonderful journey, Julia has gained experience from different cultures, hence gaining different perspectives from different angles.

Preface

This book is about Julia's heartfelt message of love between her and her mother. It is about her life growing up in Taiwan and Sydney, looking at the trials and tribulations that she endured during this time; her feelings of abandonment and social isolation, trying to work through the cultural and language barriers.

Julia has beautifully described the building of bridges and healing that has occurred with maturity and the gaining of wisdom. This has led to a higher level of understanding between Julia and her mother along with an increased ability to empathise.

J. Collier, B.Soc.Sc, MHSc (SexHlth)

"A Love Note To My Tiger Mom is a triggering point for mothers seeking to gain communication insights with their daughters"
www.alovenotetomytigermom.com

Why Mothers Should Read This Book

We all cherish how wonderfully mothers' duties are accomplished, and the unconditional love that they provide to their children. The pain of carrying babies throughout pregnancy and the fact that mothers would sacrifice everything just to ensure their babies are well fed and nurtured is admirable.

This book provides you with insights on how to bridge communication barriers to get back on track with your daughters, and also how to share life with your loved ones.

Sometimes love is not easily expressed through words, but it still can be effectively executed. You see, if there is a lack of communication, it is almost like a fully equipped electronic appliance that is simply not plugged in! How can that electronic appliance, whether it is a lamp or heater, do its job if it is not connected to the power supply? A love connection is best metaphorically explained in this way. If you love someone, do let her or him know, in the best manner you can. You never know who is around the corner collecting your love and carrying on!

My mother is a very loving person. She simply did not have the knowledge of how to express on her love until later on she joined the Tzu Chi Buddhist Foundation**, where Master Cheng Yen encourages love as the best remedy to the rest of the world. Master Cheng Yen claims that "love deprivation" is the common "disease" in this modern society. It is also the repercussion of not communicating well.

This book provides insights on how to voice loving words to your loved ones in the best appropriate manner. It gives you an understanding of how a mother took up the courage to change for the sake of her daughter. Sometimes it is not about right or wrong; it is about communication, the connection. The love stories throughout this entire book are here to share, so we know that love can take different levels beyond materialistic demand.

Love is a strong word with enormous energy. It establishes the foundation of all human being. It bonds and glues all the aspirations of people's dreams and allows them to come to fruition. It is a magical, powerful word that lies beneath our skin and no one will be able to take that away . . . but only if love is locked firmly inside your heart. That love arises from the mother, from the day she gave birth to you.

Dedication

This book is dedicated to my beloved mother, for her amazing strength in life and motherhood. She has shown the flexibility and tenacity of human strength. Thank you for believing in me and your unconditional love.

This book is also dedicated to my loving father, for all his love. I will always think of you with my smile aside. To my family; my brother, Ted Ho, and to my cousin, Max Ho, who has shared his life experience with me.

To my best friend, Noriko, who has always been walking alongside me and who provides both spiritual and mental support. We will always be holding each other's heart and will carry on with our lives in different parts of the globe. There seem to be no boundaries between us; we are so far apart but yet our hearts are tightly bound together.

To Dave and Charlene Naylor, who took me under their wings when I was desperately helpless and hopeless.

To all my beloved friends around the globe. All of YOU have come into my life (not limited to): Catherine Hung, Jeremy Lin, Sky Cheng, Josephine Lee, Rosaline Hsu, Jolene Chen, Zi Yang Lin, Phoebe Chen, Maggie Lin, Zenda Nel, Peggy, Grace Lee, Greg Foster, Justin Wang, Vivian Chou, Janice Wei, Janice Wei's mother Joyce Juan (JJ), Judy Lee (my God Sister), Penny Liao, Elaine Chen, Peter Nieh, Aimin Hale, Monica Scott, May Lee, Michael Tseng, Louis Lin, Adrian and Vera B, David Liu, Rose Sun, Ivy Yeh, Stella Kwok, Mark Thompson, Anne Hokistock, Patricia Verma, and Lorena. Thank you for being part of my life.

To Mark, thanks for your companionship during the hardest time of my life, and for being there with all ears listening.

Thank you, Eva Chui and Karen Chung, for holding my hands when I needed you most.

To all of you, your words and support have always been there with me.

To my beautiful Tzu Chi Buddhist Foundation fellow brothers and sisters. Master Cheng Yen's wisdom and words have guided me, strengthened me. My TC mother, Mother Lin, who introduced both my mother and myself in the group learning Buddha's wisdom and the great love from the Tzu Chi Foundation.

Visit Tzu Chi Buddhist Foundation at http://www.tzuchi.org/

To my fellow author group. special thanks to Darren Stehpens, who inspired me to write this book. Lynika Cruz's encouraging words and experience in writing a book. Anthea Nicholas, Pete Jensen.

To my book-writing team: Tom and Paul, who believe in this book. You have shown great companionship and have provided enormous encouragement throughout the book-writing progression.

To my fellow former colleagues, Karen Whitelock, Nastassia Lukass, Raymond Li, Jackie Lim, and Julian Milligan. To Bajaji Mani, whom with I have the honour to share the process of this book-writing journey. It is my honour to have had the great experience of working with you.

To all the readers, thank you for reading the words at this very instant. May this book's insights inspire you and your family with ways to strengthen wings to fly afar. We all have our own stories within us—for this we shall cherish life together.

CHAPTER 1
Do You Really Love Me?

In the attitude of silence of the soul finds the path in a clearer light,
and what is elusive and deceptive resoles itself into crystal clearness.
Our life is a long and arduous quest after Truth.
~Mahatma Gandhi

All my life I was sceptical if I was my mother's real daughter. I thought I might have lived in the fairy tale of the ugly duckling, who thinks he was not born by his birth mother.

When I was young, I was always throwing tantrums at my mother. To me, her attitude had always been cold. Well, not exactly cold, but she rarely listened to what I was saying. I guess when I was growing up, my mother had too many agendas on her plate, and listening to what I was trying to say seemed such a trivial thing to her. I consider that as negligence. Mundane life made her busy, and I selfishly considered that to be vulgar. I always wondered if that was my mother's characteristic—to be cold—or if she simply refused to communicate? Now I've come to realize that there are certain things you cannot change about one person, especially when she is your matriarchy mother.

I remember when I was little, I asked for good brand-new sneakers. Mother still went ahead and purchased cheapie sneakers from the street, without rationalizing why they would be good enough. I could persistently throw tantrums for three days straight, and she was good at ignoring me.

She never explained why and how; she just carried on with what she believed was right. She was stubborn and strong. She may have been right, but she never explained herself, or expressed her viewpoint. She was so focused on where she was heading, and was forgetting the rest of the family in her search for an answer. In fact, there will never be any answer or explanation—that is just the way it is in our family. My mother is the Queen Bee in the family; she dominates everything.

Later on in life she finally came up with an answer: MONEY. Everything is about money. The focal point in the family is MONEY. She derives everything from money as most Asians do. It is the reality, she taught me. But the way she executes it can be quite daunting. Every day, everything she talks about is MONEY. It can be quite debilitating sometimes, also very vulgar and boring, I thought.

There is a very interesting connection between money and love. If a child begs her mother to buy a little toy from the street, does it mean the mother loves her baby? Or is it simply an act of love? If the mother does not buy lollies for the little baby, does it mean that the mother does not love her little baby?

There are certain complexities in this scenario. If a mother is able to explain to the baby that the lolly is not good for the child's teeth and/or may cause dental decay, then she is being a good mother and is rationalizing her decision. If a mother simply purchased the lolly for the sake of keeping her child quiet, then she may cite Pavlov's theory* that by conditioning the child, her child can throw tantrums and cry out loud for lollies. In the future, the child will be constantly begging things from her mother by crying or begging—arising from the conditioning of the lollies. Incidentally, if the mother goes ahead and tells the baby that she loves her baby by giving the lolly, then the baby would then be conditioned with the expectation that lollies equate to love. Of course this is just an assumption of what would happen, but different scenarios can occur and lead to different manifestations in the child later on.

What is love? Different people have different ways of defining this profound word. Sometimes people do not fully understand the definition of love. In fact, we human beings will probably research the meaning of love for our entire lives. We all yearn for loving relationships, but sometimes we lose sight of the true meaning of love. Along the way, my mother has never stopped loving me, but she did lose sight, hence I got lost.

I often yearned for my mother's love. I was forever craving her love, her understanding, and her consent of the things I did. Deep inside, I am fearful that if I do things which she does not approve of, she will stop loving me. In reality, my mother will never stop loving me despite any of the mistakes I make. Any mother would never stop loving her children regardless of how many mistakes they made. She might not condone the mistakes I make, but she will never stop loving me.

I started hiding things from her, or doing things behind her back simply because I was fearful. She might not agree with what I do—in fact, she will always have something to say if I tell her. I would rather take risks conducting secret agendas than report to her upfront and risk being accused and rejected. There is always the possibility that she will not consent, or that she'd hold anonymous objectives against me. I could not take the risk of being myself. I was also stubborn.

In Asian culture, people tend to be more reserved with their words and feelings, especially with the word "love." Emotions are more reserved and remain in their inner self. Hence the verbal communication may be lacking, but the umbilical cord can never be cut; rather, it is stretched as far as it possibly can be. The love connection between mother and daughter never seems to end, but sometimes it needs to be acknowledged and rediscovered.

It was not until my early adulthood that I realized that all of my life, I had been searching to hear the "love" word come from my mother's mouth. It sounded quite silly, once we realized how important it was to acknowledge love, and to speak it out loud. Your loved ones have to know that you love them, and that they are loved. All it takes are the holy three words, "I Love You". My mother picked it up quite well later on, but it did sound quite quirky when one of our charity mothers from Tzu Chi Buddhist Foundation** interrogated my mother sternly as to whether she loved me or not.

It is not until later days that we realize "LOVE" is such a strong and powerful word that it almost serves a healing purpose. My mother learned to say "I love you" in every conversation she carried. If there had been any quarrels, she would always reinforce the fact that she loves me at the end of the conversation. The three magical words have exerted immense comfort and a sense of security upon me ever since.

Magically, the quarrels and misunderstandings have lessened immensely and eventually they became "communication with hasty language." Instead of fighting, my mother and I may have raised our voices a little bit higher than normal conversations, but we were able to lower our voices later. Even better, we learned to apologize and calm down later. Best of all, we will always call each other later to say "I love you" at every conversation we have had, either via phone or face-to-face. The incidents of fights have dramatically diminished. And we do not hold grudges against each other.

Now I am grown up in my mid-thirties. I feel content with the love from my mother. This solid feeling has made me a lot stronger. It is amazing how love can be so healing and it is almost like a solidifying agent, to pick up all the broken pieces and allow you to be empowered to another level. It is a simple magic power we all have, especially the magical power that arises from a mother to her child. The magical bond carries enormous power. This power that arises from one's inner self is one that no one can or will take away, because it is locked deep inside one's heart.

If you ask any mother if they love their children or not, the answer should immediately be a "Yes", but asking them to express it properly is an entirely different manner. Sometimes love can be misinterpreted by trading things we desire from our parents, hence leading to misunderstandings. Like the scenario of lolly purchasing from the mother and the little daughter, the little girl might interpret the interaction at the wrong level, ie: If the mother is not buying her the lolly, then it equates to the fact that her mother does not love her. However it may be wise for the mother to explain to her little one why she is not getting the lolly for her little girl, ie: The lolly may cause tooth decay and it is not wise to spend money on lollies . . . and so on.

My mother surely did not explain too much to me when I was little. She simply thought I was throwing tantrums. She ignored my endless crying and tearful eyes. She thought that by ignoring me long enough, I would understand later.

She continued to ignore me throughout my teenage years. She carried on whatever she thought was right without communicating with me. However, growing up in my teenage years was not as simple as her not buying me lollies. There were more than lollies when you are a teenager; there were hormones fluxing everywhere and messing around your emotions.

In her absence most of my teenage years, I got lost. My soul was lingering in limbo, and I was greatly troubled by insecurity. The feeling of hollowness turned me inside-out. On a cold winter night, I would never get warm, no matter how many layers I put on or how high I set the heater, because the chill came from the inner core of my heart.

CHAPTER 2

Who Are My Parents?

A successful marriage requires falling in love many times,
always with the same person.
~Mignon McLaughlin

B oth my parents are from Yi-Lang, a country town located on the north-eastern side of Taiwan Island. Rice was the main economic supply in Yi-Lang.

The Lang-Yang Field located in Yi-Lang provides a flat platform to harvest rice. In Asian culture, to have rice on the table means you have food supply. In many Asian languages the conventional greeting to each other is, "Have you eaten rice?" This equates to "How are you?" In the local dialogue of Hokanese, the pronunciation of "water" equates to beauty. There was an emphasis of the beauty of Yi-Lang water, hence there was a saying: "Beautiful girls arise from Yi-Lang Water." Our old ancestors were good at correlating words with natural supply. Maybe the beautiful words were spoken to encourage tenacity of living.

The living conditions back then were harsh. If the rice fields were damaged by floods, then the whole year's food supply would be in jeopardy. The year my older brother was born (1972), there was severe flood damage. To commemorate that year, my brother was named Yen-Tien, which means "to study field." In 1973 when my cousin was born (my father's younger brother's first son), the harvest was heavily affected again, and Taiwan had to borrow rice from Thailand. Because of this, my cousins was named "the rice's son," Thailand (zi-sian).

In the early years of our education we would always be taught to finish every single grain of rice which we were served. If we were to leave any of the rice unfinished, we were told that we would be marrying a spouse with spotty face; a metaphor for the unfinished rice found scattered in the bowl. I can still remember how eating rice was a ritual in the family. There was huge respect to our higher selves to provide us with food on the table. We were constantly reminded that harvesting rice was a hardship for the farmers, as the descendants of Yi-Lang.

The gratitude for rice in Asian countries is immensely immersed into the culture. In the old Chinese empire, people were always invading to gain fields from which they could harvest rice. Taiwanese, Formosa is a place where rice was the predominant economical supply. Rice was a holy crop that was heavily appreciated. To have a whole bowl of rice during my parents' childhood was considered wealth and abundance. Only the very wealthy families were able to serve rice on the table regularly.

Yi-Lang people rely heavily on the rice harvest to provide not only food but also economical supply. Since Yi-Lang is located on the eastern side of Taiwan Island, there is no natural protection from natural disasters such as the typhoon which usually comes from the eastern side of Taiwan. During typhoon season in the summer (within the period of early May and until late September), when the typhoon travelling from the eastern or south-eastern part of Taiwan, the eastern part of Taiwan would usually be the first area affected, and heavy flooding would damage the harvest of rice. Yi-Lang people rely on the higher self and the weather to provide their economical supply.

My mother was the daughter of a wealthy landlord in the countryside of Taiwan, Yi-Lang. My mother was born in 1948 in the year of the rat, according to Chinese zodiac. People born during the year of the rat are usually very active and love to pursue properties, as is the rat's habit (ie: the rats love going around digging holes to make themselves comfortable within their zone of home). These people live on busy schedules and never stop.

My mother behaves very much like a rat, but like one which is a bit chubby. You see, when a rat is a little bit overweight, it means she cannot run very fast. This is my mother. She is not a very fast-paced person, but she is always patient with things. She hardly ever raises her temper. She is very slow-motioned and will always react a few seconds later than she is supposed to. She is a funny rat, I tell you. Sometimes I giggle about her slow motion, and sometimes it drives me insane. You can almost picture a big chubby rat trying to run while struggling at the same time. This scene can sometimes be quite interesting to picture. The great thing about her is that she works hard and never gives up. It probably takes longer for her to achieve her goal, but she is tenacious. She hardly looks back but is moving forward constantly.

After my grandmother gave birth to my mother, my granny suffered from severe fatigue syndrome and was unable to take care of my infant mother. My mother was fostered approximately 2 to 3 kilometres from her birth parents. Hence, my mother had adopted her foster parents' last name of Lin instead of her birth parents' last name, Liu. My mother's foster mother adored my mother. There were three generations from the foster family who really loved my mother: the foster parents, the grandfather, and the great grandmother. My mother was very lucky to be loved by her whole foster family. According to my mother, the three generations would save all the drumsticks for her alone to enjoy during the festive season. So if the family had slaughtered two chickens for that festive season, then she would end up having the total of four drumsticks to eat. She would have secretly counted the right numbers of drumsticks under the table with a firm smile on her face. I remember her proudly telling me that her mathematic talent arose from that counting.

She must have learned unconditional love from her foster family, learning the fact that a mother would sacrifice her personal favour for her little child. My mother always told me that although her foster parents were very poor, she was very much loved by them. The little hut in the country was very much filled with love and childhood memories, and the warmth will always linger in my mother's heart. Even though my mother's foster parents were very poor, she was brought up with lots of intense love.

The bond between my mother and her foster mother was very strong. Even when my mother have grown at the age of eighteen and had left home for Taipei to study, she would always return home and sleep with her foster mother. My mother absolutely loved the sensation of lying next to her beloved mom. Unfortunately her foster mother died at the age of fifty from cervical cancer. Both my brother and I never got to meet her. Years after Foster Granny died, my mother still talked about her with tears.

As the foster family was very poor, my mother's foster granny had to go outside of town to serve as a maid for wealthy families. The foster father was a gambler, so he was unable to provide for the family with stable finances. He would probably earn a bit of money but gambled all of it away. Learning from her foster father, my mother swore never to gamble; she loathed gambling.

In those days the government graded poverty families in order to provide financial support. The foster parents' family was considered to be in the secondary poverty level. Secondary poverty comes after primary poverty, meaning even though they were not the poorest at the time, they were poor enough to receive financial support from the government.

Due to her family's financial situation, my mother had to start working at the age of thirteen, straight out of primary school. She had to carry heavy shoulder poles (a tool that is made from mature bamboo sticks, with a barrel hung off at each side for balance). Using shoulder poles, she had to carry goods to the next village to sell merchandise. She sold fruits and vegetables, depending on which ones were profitable. During the Chinese New Year, while others were enjoying the festive season, she would also start a small shop selling small gimmicks or firecrackers to pay for her tuition or living costs for the following year.

Although her birth parents were reasonably wealthy to be able to harvest rice, they did not provide full financial support of my mother's education or living expenses. They told my mother, "Once you are fostered, you belong to the other family but not us." Those were quite harsh statements for my mother to hear.

My mother still occasionally went back and asked her birth parents for financial support. In return she had to work in the field with her other brothers and sisters. The work was quite difficult. My mother was clumsy and she was always behind her siblings in the tasks. Her birth parents eventually agreed to pay half of her tuition, and my mother had to earn the rest for herself. On top of that, she also needed to earn her own living costs.

My mother was very much traumatized by her family's poor situation. She was under oath that she will never go back to poverty again. I remember one day she told me with tearful eyes that she would never allow her family members to suffer from poverty. To achieve this, she feels that being thrifty and getting prepared is the best way to live.

My father grew up in a big family. My grandfather was a governor during the time when Taiwan was colonized by Japan. He spoke perfect Japanese and worked for the Japanese government. When the Taiwanese government (KMT Party) came to Taiwan in 1947, the political issue became critical. Prior to that, the Japanese government had colonized Taiwan for fifty years. There were people who had gotten used to the Japanese government, as the Japanese had a very strict way governing people. To some extent, it was easy for the people to follow the rules because they were quite clear-cut and the grey area was comparatively small. The civilians received a harmonized and steady life without having to worry about law violations as long as people behaved. Up to this point, the people in my parents' generation or above who were educated under Japanese system still hold good memories of the "good old days." The days were simpler without too many political issues and unanswered questions. The Taiwanese culture is very much influenced by Japan. Most of the Taiwanese are exposed to Japanese culture and know how to speak a little bit of it.

Well, my father's background story involved a few political issues. My grandfather was a governor in the Japanese days. He achieved a relatively high ranking. In the peak of his time, his family owned one side of the street of Rong-Dong CBD (a small city in Yi-Lang). It is likely that my grandfather did well acquiring all the properties on the street, and the family was quite wealthy when my father was little. In 1947, after the KMT Party, the Taiwanese government came to Taiwan to take over, and my grandfather's social status was adversely affected. My father was five at the time.

Both of my grandparents got remarried, as they had each lost a spouse. They remarried so that they would have someone to look after the family together with. My father was the eldest son of my grandparent's second marriage. Since he was the eldest son of my grandmother's second marriage, he inherited the responsibility to look after the younger ones: his younger brother, my uncle.

My granny has a very interesting name, Gien Ho; it literally means "thrifty." As the extended family's size was getting quite big (with approximately ten people in the household), my granny had to start a business in the local market to earn a living to feed the family. My father, being my granny's eldest son, he had to follow in her footsteps and work with her.

They were selling all kinds of fruits in the local market, and the business was quite good. Being good at merchandizing locally at a young age, my father had acquired good skills in selecting fruits and vegetables. According to my father, they were able to make gross profit of NTD 1,000 per day, which measured very well in those days. The tuition standard in those days was approximately NTD 300 per semester. However, since the size of the family was quite large, all of the money earned went to support general living expenses. There were limited amounts that my granny could put away for savings.

Due to the changeover of two different governments, my grandfather lost his high social rank. In order to numb himself from the loss of his high rank, he got himself drunk every day. Amazingly he was able to get home in one piece while drunk and then collapse. Seeing this dramatic change of the family's situation, insecurity sank into my father's mind tremendously.

One night my grandfather was drunk again and after he got home, he fell from the second floor and passed away in my father's arms. My father was seventeen; it must have been an enormous shock to my father in his youth. Like most Asian men, my father is quite reserved with his feelings; he never mentions his emotions to his family. There is always this suspicion that the unfinished business resides in the dark corner of my father's mind, and there reside some elements of resentment.

At the age of eighteen when he was in the final year of finishing his college degree, my father dropped out of college right before completing his degree. There has always been suspicion that he did not finish his schooling because of his mental state. This was never mentioned or worded out loud by my father. He had always kept his youth a secret to us, until later on when I pieced it together from my mother like a jigsaw puzzle.

My parents met at work. When my father was pursuing my mother, he was very aggressive. He absolutely adored her. He had agreed with everything my mother had proposed if they were to be married, including the fact that my father was to take my mother's maiden name instead of her taking his name. So when they had their first son, he would have inherited the last name from my mother's foster family, Lin, not from my father, Ho.

My mother requested this because her foster family had no son to carry on the family name, Lin. So she had to take the responsibility to carry on the family name. My father was obsessed with my mother, to whom he agreed without hesitation, even forgetting to consult with my granny prior to marriage. He was really in love. I guess love is blind.

When my parents first got married, they lived with my uncle and his wife together with my granny. This arrangement was intended to bond the family together and to also save on the rental cost as well.

My older brother was born one year after my parents got married. As a twist of my parents' love story, my brother ultimately did not carry my mother's last name. He was the eldest grandson of my grandmother, and my granny would not allow my brother to take any other surname but Ho, my father's surname. In consideration of my granny who had heart conditions, my mother eventually compromised and gave in.

My father was later on diagnosed with unstable mood swing. His mental state was never steady, and he could get very excited over certain things and then he would get very depressed for a period of time. According to my mother, there was a predictable cycle when he was in his forties and fifties. It was easier to formulate a proper way to deal with my father's mental state.

His unstable mood swing started after we moved out from my uncle's place. When my father was diagnosed, people pointed fingers at my mother. My relatives claimed that moving out from my granny's place must have caused the mental issues. Well, I have no way to correlate the two; how could my father's illness have been affected by the move? I guess when bad things happen, someone or something usually has to be blamed? Nevertheless, it was actually these mental fluctuations that allowed my father to be quite creative in running a business.

When I was five, my father had his first onset of unstable mood swing. He was unconscious for a couple of days without proper reason. The doctor could not provide a proper prognosis. At that time, people in Taiwan did not have a proper understanding of severe unstable mood swing. They labeled this illness as "crazy" or had some other sort of twisted idea about it. The hospital ward had its own special rules: Peoples' belongings had to be left outside of the ward before going into it. IDs were carefully checked, and there was a security door at the gate so no one without permission could enter in the building.

I remember I was taken to the hospital to see him with my mother, but since my mother was the caregiver, and I was too small or too young, they would not allow me to go in. I had to wait for another aunty to come and collect me to see him. I was crying alone outside of the ward. It was lonesome and scary. By the time I was collected and went to my father's bedside to see him, he was unconscious. No one could wake him. My mother had asked me to call my father, and miraculously he reciprocated. He only responded to my calling. It was obvious that my father's love towards me was enormously strong and intense.

Due to my father's illness, the business could not continue steadily. My father's mental state was going in cycles, up and down. Sometimes he could be very excited with things and that could carry him throughout the whole process of the particular projects he was working on. And then he would go through cycles of a very low, depressed mode where it would be lucky he would get out of bed and work.

I was considered a lucky star in the family. In the Asian culture it is said that when you have a baby boy born in the family, his responsibility is to carry on the family's name. The baby girl, on the other hand, is supposed to bring the family monetary luck. I seemed to be the one who brought the family monetary luck.

My mother had always wanted a girl. When I was born, my parents were blissfully enjoying the new member of the family. I can still remember when I was little; my mother used to call me from a distance and asked me to go to her for a huge hug. I can still remember the warmth of my mother's arms. It is a beautiful memory encoded in my mind, my childhood.

My parents started a business not long before I was born. As mentioned before, I was the lucky monetary one. I brought prosperity to the family. The business was of relatively small size. My mother was the finance holder in the family and my father was responsible for going out to search for projects to generate income. My father could be quite creative with business; he was a very smart man. By nature my father was a happy person in general. However, I suspect that there was always unfinished business in my father's mind that haunted him. So when depression came and haunted him, those sad memories came back and bit him badly.

The business paid the bill, but did not provide continual income. This was partly because the nature of the business was project-based, and partly because of my father's illness. The business could provide a lump sum income at times, and then it would be months before the next project created income. My father worked closely with military sections and with the government. He had a very good relationship with the people working in the military section.

Due to the nature of the business, my mother's financial strategy was to save every single penny earned to ensure financial security. She was a great saver. I have never encountered a thriftier person than her in my life. Whenever the company is earning a large sum of money, she would either pay off the house mortgage or go ahead and purchase another one, if she could afford it. Over the years she managed to accumulate a few properties, but no cash at hand. She considered properties to lead to monetary assets, whereas cash could be easily spent and disappear.

In the first couple of years after the onset of my father's health condition, the family's financial situation became quite critical. My father was hospitalized a couple of times throughout the years. When he became quite sick the first time, my mother had a business to run, two kids to feed, a mortgage to pay off, and a sick husband. Additional drama came when the company staff saw the situation of the company owner and they resigned under the fear of not being paid on time. My mother was left alone with all these responsibilities. Without much financial support from others, imagine how stressful it would have been for her.

My mother told me that she felt truly hopeless, but she could not collapse. She simply had too many responsibilities on her shoulders. When my father was going through the cycles, she told herself that she had to sleep to keep the days going, so she did. Her strong-willed mind told her to get a good night's sleep. Thankfully she has always been good at sleeping. She never brings her stress with her when she goes to sleep; that is the main way that she keeps herself nice and healthy.

Back in those days, people did not have the right perceptions of unstable mood swing. This was labeled as "craziness" or "madness." Sadly, these labels were given to my father. Both my parents did not know how to confront this illness, and the two of them were quite upset. I can still remember how, as a kid, I saw my parents so much in love, and they were hugging each other. My father apologetically said to my mother, "I am sorry that I am sick." They both cried. I was five.

All of these uncertainties contribute to my mother's thrifty behaviour. Although I do not totally agree with it, I am very inspired by her determination to save. She is determined to leave at least one property to her kids (both my brother and myself) for us reside in, so we will only need to earn our living without having to worry about rent or paying off a mortgage when we grow up. She has achieved this with every single cell of her determination.

My mother has managed to live within her means and, of course, she has no idea what Louis-Vuitton, Gucci, or the rest of the luxury bags and fashion designers mean at all. She once told me that it would be such a luxury to go and buy and enjoy a cup of coffee from the café. That was her ultimate definition of luxury.

It can be quite difficult to live with her, since she simply does not spend. When you try to live under the current norm of life, she will reluctantly tell you off or scold you. Today, although she is more than comfortable, she still lives well within her means. It became her second nature.

CHAPTER 3
My Brother and My Childhood

There is a garden in every childhood,
an enchanted place where colours are brighter,
the air is softer, and the morning more
fragrant than ever again.
~Elizabeth Lawrence

My childhood was a mixture of happiness and resentment. My parents worked very hard to support the family. They also made the effort to provide us the best they could afford. Both my brother and I went to schools locally. We lived in a very good area in the central part of Taipei, in an education zone where all the good schools were located. The schools we attended were amongst the top-ranked schools in the municipal Taipei. We went to the primary school that only took us ten minutes to walk to, and the secondary school took approximately fifteen minutes by foot.

I was educated to be independent at very young age. I remember my mother only came and collected me from school on the first and second days. The first day she showed me how to walk home and the second day she taught me how to take the bus to my parents' office. Thereafter I needed to be independent. I needed to learn how to use the key to our apartment. I needed to remember my keys, because otherwise I would not be able to enter my home in my parents' absence.

My brother was four years my senior. He would look after me when he finished school. However, he usually finished school later than I did, so there were times I was alone in the apartment without any adult supervision. It can be quite lonesome and challenging to stay at home alone as a child. Thinking back, I may have developed the acquired independence from as young as seven or eight years of age.

I remember my brother and I used to do lots of little things to entertain ourselves. We had a local shop that fills my childhood memories. They supplied all kinds of colourful lollies, bubbles to blow, and little games with a little money attainable. My brother and I loved that shop. There were things we loved to explore outside of our schoolings. Like most children, exploring things out of our parents' supervision was quite adventurous.

To be honest, my parents were quite liberal with the things they allowed us to do, apart from being so tight financially. I was able to go to my friend's place or sleep over without too much hassle. As my parents were seldom there after school, I often asked my friends from the neighbourhood to come over and play with me. There were lots of things we could do without too much constraint. I remember once when we were asked to make aboriginal dresses from different kinds of materials. My friend and I used strings to make ourselves a skirt—one of those Hawaiian skirts you would swing and turn with the rustling sounds.

At the age of ten years or so, my mates and I would also go to the local grocery shops and get foodstuff to eat. It was quite fun to play around with our neighbours. However I always had this loneliness and resentment at the fact that I was unable to see my parents after work, and I had to look after myself, to be independent. When you are forced to learn things, it gets difficult. When you do not understand *why* and *how*, it leaves a huge question mark in your mind.

My photographic memory helped me to be a good student. When my brother was trying to recite words from a textbook, he was reading it several times, and I was the one who ended up remembering all the words without knowing what they meant. I was that good!

I was always studious, behaved well, followed what I was told at school, and was very punctual when handing in my homework. I had very high self-esteem and never misbehaved. I remember one of my primary school teachers was quite strict; she would always punish us if we forgot to bring our homework or textbooks to school. I was always careful not to violate rules from either the school or from the teacher. However, somehow there is a rebellious side of me that needs to get out. The rebellious Julia was eventually liberated later on in my life when things did not work out the way I desired.

CHAPTER 4

The Interlocking Fourteen-Year-Old

Education consists mainly of what we have unlearned.
~Mark Twain

At the age of fourteen, I was facing enormous academic pressure in Taiwan. My school teacher was a very strict teacher—a mathematical devil coach. She would have you reciting all the algebra formulae and ask you to remember everything and expect you to score 100%. If you did not achieve the standard expected, then you were likely to be punished. There were several forms of punishments, including being hit with a stick on the hands or on the bottom.

It is undeniable that one wants to try to avoid being hurt, right? However, if you try to avoid being hit by the stick, then the teacher is likely to only hit you harder. The more atrocious thing happens when you wear an extra layer underneath your skirt; the teacher claims that extra layer protects you from being hurt. Well, come to think of it, what is wrong with protecting yourself from being hurt? I can never come to a reasonable explanation for all these punishments. All I know is that our teacher was a very aggressive teacher, she would focus entirely on her students' academic results, and her dedication was highly regarded at our school.

We never got to go home on time. She had all my classmates stay after school for "after-school care," so we were able to spend more time studying and being supervised by her or by the rest of our classmates. There were always tight schedules telling us what to do for after-school hours, and dinners would be catered by outside parties so that we were property fed. We used to call her "Devil Coach" at school. She was energetic and so focused on what she was trying to achieve, and she did score our team members well, that was for sure. Most of my classmates were from well-educated families—children of school teachers, doctors, lawyers, successful businessmen, etc. The families of my classmates all had medium to high social status. Of course, our parents expected us to score high academically.

The main structure of the Junior high school system (Years seven through nine) in Taiwan was different in those days (the 1990's). The classes were basically segregated into normal school classes and "good classes." Each class had a Guidance Teacher who was responsible for organizing all of the activities of the class, including the sports activities, competitions, and academic activities involved to enhance the students' academic results. The "good classes" were the ones with a highly capable Guidance Teacher who was able to train the students to achieve outstanding scores. Usually these classes were organized intrinsically from the close relationships behind the scenes.

The parents of high social status had ways to get connected with the school administrative system, so they were able to put their kids into the "good class". Usually the students in the good class had better chances to score higher than ordinary class students, and they were able to get into good senior high schools (year ten to twelve), ultimately entering prestigious universities. To be able to get into a good university and to achieve high scores seemed to be the major mission of the Taiwanese parents. Higher education means better jobs in the future, which is the very myth that Asian parents believe.

According to ancient Chinese saying, "Tens of thousands are all inferior and suffer, but only studying enhances prestigious ranks." In the ancient Chinese era, the only way for the commoner to become a governor was to attend an annual examination held by the government. If one scored the highest academically, then he would be elected to become a governor or politician. A governor or politician in the ancient Chinese empire was considered to be a prestigious career in which you were exposed to luxury and, most importantly, to POWER. This crucial value has passed on to generations of Chinese descendents. Therefore almost every parent would strive for their kids to score high academically as part of the security blanket for future jobs. In Asia, money is such an important issue, and having good academic results somehow interlocks with monetary security.

I question whether a high academic score guarantees a good career path later on in life. There are lots of successful entrepreneurs who did not even finish university, such as Steve Jobs, Bill Gates, and Mark Zuckerberg. They still went on to be extremely successful in their amazing career paths. Well, I am not trying to challenge the old traditional education system; there is certainly a strong demand for higher education, and traditionally it created the passing ticket for employment in the society. However, it is not the only ticket to acquire a secure career path. There were people who spent a lot of time trying to achieve high academic results, but who lost perspective of what the value of those academic achievements is. The core thinking of *why*, *what* and *how* has been lost along the way, and sadly there are people doing certain courses of what is best for their future careers, but they've forgotten if they are really interested in these careers or if they are even good at them or not.

Life is all about choices. I was lucky to be able to make choices at the age of thirteen, and I chose the strictest guidance teacher of the whole year. I was helping a teacher who governed the allocations of students to different classes during summer break. As a trade-off, the teacher allowed me to choose any class I wanted. At that point in time, my mother had already used her connections with the school administration to put me into one of the good classes. But I went on to choose the strictest one, taught by my teacher, Ms Jing. Ms Jing was known for her heroic record of taking all her students on to score high. She was a female but was able to take up a male teacher's job.

She was always energetic and vibrant. Her focus and her passion for teaching is admirable, but her way of teaching was not. She took every opportunity for her students to score high. She went through all the cramming materials to coach her students, and had all of us kept at the school under her guidance to study. We were forced to study. We were taught to study, but we were not taught to think. To be obedient to her guidance and not able to think on our own was quite detrimental. When some of our old classmates gathered together later on in our young adulthood, they could not cope with the thought of even reciting those old days. The only thing we did was study. I was in her class for two years, year seven and eight. I never remember seeing daylight in those two years. I had to leave home before sunrise, and then was welcomed by the moonlight on the way home.

I suffered tremendously, both mentally and physically, in those days. I loathed my teacher. All I wanted was to go home early and have a bit of leisure. However, it was not possible. I was always complaining in my diary to my teacher. She knew that I was complaining, but she also knew her goal was to get the class score as high as possible. That was her main priority. My rebellious character began strongly fighting against her, and more importantly, I was fighting against myself.

Although I scored well academically with the average of mid 90's, my physical health was declining. With all the extreme stress encountered, I was experiencing excruciating stomach pain. I lost four kilos in one week, simply because I could not eat. I would bite a little and stop as my stomach was churning painfully. All the health examinations showed I was okay, but I simply could not eat. Even the amount of water I drank was scarce. I could only drink one quarter of a cup (equivalent to approx 100cc) per day. My eyesight was also depreciating. My glasses were getting thicker and thicker. My parents were really worried.

One day, my father came home and told us that we had the opportunity to immigrate to Australia, as our application had been granted. At that point I was not aware what was ahead of us. All I knew was I had an opportunity to go overseas to study, and I needed to speak English. From then on, I started picturing all the academic works I was learning in English. I would need to translate all the physics, mathematics, and chemistry into English terminology. Of course, as a fourteen-year-old girl, the future was so much of a mystery and adventure. Australia? A continent full of koala and kangaroos, I asked myself?

Seven days before my fourteenth birthday, my mother took me to Australia to study. Throughout my years growing up in Taiwan, I have always exhibited independent characteristics in my mother's eyes. She knew I could score reasonably high at school, and she knew I was capable of looking after myself, but at the age of fourteen? How did she have faith in me?

Well, I did survive my teenage years without too much of her presence, and eventually I remained in one piece. There were elements of resentment residing within me for a long time, and they lingered there until my mother finally acknowledged her love to me. The education of love is continuous and it probably takes all of our lives to learn. The main key is to never be thrifty with words of love to your love ones. There is nothing to be shamed about in expressing your love and caring to your love ones.

CHAPTER 5

The Calendar, Lonely Teenage Years

I hated every minute of training, but I said,
"Don't quit. Suffer now and live the rest
of your life as a champion."
~Muhammad Ali

I often wonder, what do others do at the ages of sixteen through eighteen? This is the age when your hormones start to shoot from nowhere and there is always this uncontrollable temper that is yet to skyrocket. Unfortunately this is the period of time I would really like to eliminate from my memory. Sometimes I wish there was a delete button in my imaginary computer head, and that I could simply press the button and it is gone, gone completely. That part of my life contained so many sorrows that even thinking about it can be distressful.

The most debilitating part of it was that there was nobody to turn to, no one to understand it. It was very lonely to go through that pathway alone, especially when I was a teenager. It seems that all the obstacles triple their hardships when it happens during teenage years. There were times I felt as though I was quitting life. The sense of instability and insecurity made me suffer tremendously. Those were the attributes that could destroy one person, and they almost destroyed me. I survived because there is this inner voice guiding me. It is better to be challenged when you are still young; it is easier to bounce back at a young age. I will always remember this quote, "The Footprint".

I burst into tears when I read this quote years ago, especially the last three sentences: *"During your times of trials and suffering, when you see only one set of footprints, it was that I carried you."* It was that I carried you. It was though as this had been voiced to me via some sort of supernatural power; my guardian angel or Buddha was carrying me during the hardest time of my life. Now I still get emotional when I read this quote at times. My tears are filled with both appreciation and love—love from someone above.

I have a very different sensation now I read it than when I read it years ago. Years ago when I was reading it, I was feeling extremely hopeless and trying to get through those dark hours with tremendous struggle. Now, when I am reading it, my tears are filled with appreciation. I tell myself, "I DID it!"

Somehow there must be a higher power (either Buddha, God or a Guardian Angel. I am a Buddhist, however I love the idea of a guardian angel) up there guiding me and helping me through all these hardships. Miraculously I passed all the tests, one by one. I may have stumbled with a bleeding knee or broken ankles, but at the end I managed to stand up with pride and joy.

There were incidents I will always remember, and the scary part of it is that they come back and haunt me with those vivid feelings—the intense feelings of fear, sorrow, and loneliness. After all these incidents were all over, it was the fearful moments left that you have to deal with emotionally. The psychological part is that YOU are the ONLY member who partakes in the scene. Whoever comes into your life and helps you to go through that process can only partake as an onlooker; they can only help in the process of guiding or comforting you. YOU are the ONLY person who has to go through that pathway and take that big step out of that zone of fear, or out of any other negative emotions involved.

The Calendar

Throughout almost eight years of living in Sydney, my mother came and went in the meantime. In the initial years, she had to stay here to fulfil her citizenship. In those days, it was necessary to stay here for two years within five years of validity of permanent residency (PR). Due to my father's mental state and the family's financial status, she had to fly between Sydney and Taipei. I remember she had a calendar with her on which she counted the days she had to stay here to fulfil the residency—we called them the "immigration jailing period." She used to cross the days out one by one. It made a huge impact on me, this sense of not being wanted. It hurts to have known my mother had to leave me alone here. It hurts.

Endless Drama in the House

There was a small hill right before you reached my old house. It seemed to be the final hill that you would have to climb up to reach your destination. I have always been quite bad at sports, but I tried to work on it. It was my very first experience to bike in Sydney. In a hills district where there are ups and downs, it might not be a great idea to bike. I guess I was adventurous. My neighbour lent me a bike and I rode on it. The first time became the last time in my life in which I would bike in Sydney; I fell over when I was going down the hill. My right leg was badly wounded with a huge scar. It took several years for the scar to fade away, as well as for it to fade in my heart. I suppose if it was just an ordinary fall with a bit of scratches on your leg, it would not have been a great deal, but I remember that I was so alone and had to walk a few streets away, including climbing up and down the hills limping, filled with a feeling with mixture of physical pain, loneliness and a bit of helplessness.

The summer I was fifteen, again, my mother was away. That summer was made most memorable to me as I had to travel six places throughout the entire hot weather. Since I was not independent enough, my mother tried to figure out who should look after me when she was away. I had to go and stay with a couple of friends in the neighbourhood as I was too young to live alone. Sometimes my friend came over and stayed with me, but not permanently. So I was going forward and backwards to my various friends' places, one after the other. One of the six places I went to was a summer camp. They were lots of outdoor activities to get involved, but when you are feeling so lonely, it seemed hard for me to be outspoken or mingle with people. Apart from that, I was feeling inferior as my English was not exactly fluent at the time, and I resented the sense of not having my family around.

I finally made myself feel at home living in the house my mother bought. We had a whole lot of roses in front of our garden, and when they blossomed the scent was beautiful. My mother used to go and pick up roses from the garden and put them in the house so we could enjoy the beautiful smell. After I came home from my extensive travelling, I learned from my mother and picked up roses from the garden. But all of these bugs came out of nowhere. I was bitten all over my body. It was a horrific experience. I had to go and get a pest bomb from the supermarket to have the whole room sprayed. I washed the bed sheets and had to sleep on the couch for a few days before I knew it was clear in my bed. From then on, I never picked up the roses in the garden, no matter how lovely they smelled.

The winter following that summer, I got really sick. I had a flu that lasted almost six weeks. I was sneezing, coughing, and had endless fatigue. I remember that winter being especially cold for me. It was up to the point that I had excruciating pain with my lungs due to the heavy coughing. Finally I recuperated from my cold and then subsequent drama came along. They say that when there is bad luck, it comes in threes. Well, for me the drama had only ever come under sixes. There were five incidents including my six weeks of endless flu. Should I consider myself lucky that it went just below the multitude of three, six? I laughed at myself.

I usually walked to school during my high school years. One day while on my way to school, I was trying to get there faster by running with little steps, and I felt over. I sprained my right ankle and subsequently hurt my left knee. Ouch! I know it was painful. I could not go further and my friend went back and asked for help from my mother. Luckily my mother was in Sydney at the time. She quickly came over and rescued me, and I had a ride to school that day.

The following few days when I was putting chlorine into the pool, guess what? I fell over again! So now I had two wounded knees! You would imagine that I was walking in slow motion during that period of time. I remember that by the time the second recess bell rang, I had only managed to walk a few steps down. Well, with two damaged knee, what more could you expect? What was next, you might ask.

My mother had to go back to Taiwan sometime during October that year. I would have to go back to Taiwan by December that year during school holidays. So after my mother went home, I had a sty in my eye! It was very painful, but the general practitioner would not remove it. They said that it would go away, just like that. Well, it did not. I was supposed to go to Japan to visit my best friend prior going back to Taiwan. I had to delay my flight of going back to Japan, and went back to Taiwan first. As soon as I landed in Taipei, I was taken to the hospital and had the sty removed. I remember taking the flight with my right eye swollen like a walnut. It was not only an unpleasant look, but it was very painful.

When I recount my life back in my teenage years, the horrific scenes still vividly play in front of me as if it were just like yesterday. Thankfully back in those days, Sydney was a very peaceful place and I lived in a suburban quiet area. Well, the area is still a peaceful and quiet area now, but I can still remember all those disastrous memories.

My next door neighbour was an old Australian bloke who spent most of his time in the garden and worked hard. Fred was his name. According to my mother, Fred had a Chinese girlfriend when he was young; that was why he was very fond of my mother. My mom spent most of her time in the garden when she was around in the property and Fred did the same thing. The friendship between the pair of them bonded so well, and Fred claims my mother was a genius as she always came up with various creative ideas of how to work on our garden in the most economical way.

Our Sydney house exerted enormous sadness in my teenage years. It was already approximately thirty years old when we purchased the property. There were constantly things to be repaired, including the hideous swimming pool. You had to put chlorine in the pool every one to two days just to ensure that the algae were out of sight. The garden was enormous and there were constantly blue tongues (a type of lizard who has a blue tongue) coming out of somewhere to say hello to you. As a city girl, I was never able to cope with the huge property on my own. I was almost petrified residing with all these wild animals or creatures outside of the house.

There were numerous times when I complained to my mother and begged her to do something about it, i.e. to size down to a smaller property where there was not much demand to look after the garden. My mother never listened. She figured that it would cost a bit of money to change over properties and there was absolutely no need. She refused to listen to me. She did nothing to change the circumstances but carried on whatever she thought was the most appropriate route. She was very stubborn and appeared to be absolutely "cold-blooded" towards my words to her. Those cold attitudes absolutely hurt me.

She also ignored others' suggestions. To this date, I am still amazed at how stubborn she can be to carry on whatever she thought was right, without considering all the repercussions. She simply thought I was behaving like a teenager! The fact that she put me in deep dismay was very distressful. I was never able to get out of that haunted place during my teenage years.

In my high school years, I struggled in associating with peers; simply no one was able to picture what I went through. They perceived me as an odd creature and I dissociated from them. I was lonely, and lonely and lonely. The despair haunted me for a long time and I always thought my schoolmates from high school teased me in those days, when, in fact, I was the one who was unable to express myself. Sometimes when you have sorrow encoded in your eyes, people can feel it, and that makes you unapproachable.

I was also very much victimized and traumatized by those years of sad experiences. It took me several years to understand the meaning of victimization and traumatisation. By understanding and recognizing the process of the two, it was then easier to untangle the constraints of both victimization and traumatisation. It is like battling with your illness: the best way to approach the illness is to live peacefully with it, but not trying to fight against it. Then you find a way to strategically work on it.

When I think back on those sorrowful days, I still see myself with hollow eyes. I was simply sad. My heart was torn and was constantly seeking for understanding. At that point, no one was able to understand. NO ONE. It almost appeared to me that I was the only person left in this world, and the absolute chill and hollowness haunted me endlessly.

Years after I came back to Sydney, when I do have the chance to catch up with the old friends of mine, they simply had no recollection of what had happened. I think they may think I was an odd person, a loner. Of course there were competitions between my classmates and myself. I was doing reasonably well considering my English level was not exactly perfect. That put a few competitions and quarrels into the group. The crucial key with my teenage years was that I was going through with the confusion and misunderstanding with everyone else, BUT I had NO ONE to turn to. That was the lonely part. My other classmates had their family support. All I had was a full bricked wall surrounding me and an empty house with no life.

I tried to write to my parents overseas, detailing my loneliness. My brother's advice to me was that I should really learn to grow up and be independent. I should not express all my personal feelings to my parents as those words would make them worry. How sad it was to have no family with you in the teenage years and then to be told to reserve all these feelings to yourself. Well, those negative feelings came back later on and bit me enormously.

My mother sub-rented the house to other people who also came from Taiwan. She did it with two reasons. One was to keep the family finances going, and the other was to have someone to look after me. Things did not go as well as my mother had originally planned. They were strangers to me, and always had misunderstandings or adjustments to be done. Well, they are not my family members, and the total intrusion of privacy was not a pleasant experience.

There were quarrels and misunderstandings with the tenants. When the tenants moved out from the property, my mother would start scolding me, telling me it was my fault that they moved out. She blamed me and said that I was not easy to get along with. Every single word she said imprinted in my mind until this day, and sadly enough she totally forgot about it in the recent conversation I had with her. Maybe there is a delete button in her mind that she managed to utilize that to wipe out all the words she had said?! Her words were harsh and detrimental, it was like a knife directly cutting through my heart.

My mother had the reputation of being thrifty in the community, and when she left, I was the one left to confront all the finger pointing. I guess if I were to be less sensitive, maybe things could go a bit better. The Asian community was small, and everyone knew everyone in the neighbourhood. They all knew I was my mother's daughter—the strange little one who was left alone here by her mother, and had a bit of strange loner temper.

I can still remember one Christmas when I was invited to my friends' place to celebrate such festive seasons. A neighbour of mine who was also from Taiwan whom I call Uncle (we were not blood-related, but usually it is polite to call someone at your mother's generation uncle in Asian culture), pointed a finger at me saying, "Julia, you are such a pitiable little girl." He meant what he said, he sympathized with my situation and that I was left alone here in a foreign country. He never meant to hurt me, but he was not considerate enough to know that my pride was badly hurt.

Even if I am such a pitiable little girl, I still deserve some respect, I said to myself. This finger pointing act hurt; it almost felt like someone stabbing you right through your heart with a sharp knife. I ran out of the door after that incident. I simply could not cope. My eyes were filled with sad tears. I knew my mother had her standpoint. Even though I knew what my mother did was not exactly appropriate, she was trying her best to balance everything in the family, and the family's finances were the top priority in my mother's eyes.

When the tenants moved out, it meant the loss of income. My mother would freak out on me. The other thing she would freak out on me was the fact that there were repairs to be done to house. I remember there were constantly things to repair: the stove was broken, the swimming pool filter needed replacement, and the lawn needed to be mowed, and there were plumber works to be done, etc. They all cost money, and when she was informed, she freaked out. She shouted at me for not looking after the property. I was only sixteen when all these happened; how could I be responsible for all of this? I had no words to defend myself.

My mother's sense of insecurity affected me badly. I was severely insecure. Sometime later I discussed all these matters to my mother, and of course she could not remember that she had scolded me. All she could remember was that it was expensive to live in Australia. So she rolled her sleeves up to save every single cent she could to keep the family finances going.

My impression of the pool was quite uniquely unpleasant. It was an old pool, and from time to time it needed repair. One day the pool needed some repairs as the filter was old. The tradesman that came to fix up the pool was a huge six feet tall! This man was a very tall man and he had moustache on him. When he arrived at my place, he used the swimming pool water to clean his face when the water was not even clean! Yes, I was the only person in the property to confront this huge big Caucasian man. It was quite frightening to have a sixteen-year-old girl facing the tradesman. I must admit, I was quite terrified!

During a rain-pouring summer day, I even found a huge pelican at the back of my garden. I guess that gigantic bird was passing by and thought it was a pond, but in fact it was a pool at the back of my garden! Oh my, I was totally petrified. That huge beak with a large set of wings almost shook a heart attack out of me. Up until today, I can still feel the pelican's eyes gazing at me. I remember it quite vividly that I was unable to approach the pool for a few days after that! All these unpleasant experiences told me to avoid the swimming pool as much as I could. Later in the years, I learned to develop swimming as a hobby, but never in that pool. All this drama kept me from ever swimming in the pool.

When I was eighteen, I finally stood up to my mother, saying that I was unable to live with tenants, since there were too many incidents happening in the house and I just did not want things to reoccur over and over again. She finally consented to have me alone in the house. That brought another major issue—I felt very lonely but I would rather be alone; sharing things with others bothered me even more.

The solitude framed me significantly to be a loner. I did not like to be approached by strangers or people that I felt would be harmful me. I was very vulnerable and susceptible to my surroundings. I had a fractured soul. I remember one day I attended a gathering from my charity group. The group was advocating how to enhance relationships between parents and their children. I was in their children's generation. The speaker had asked everyone who had attended to go home and tell their families how much they love them. I knew that I had no one to turn to when I would go home. I had only the cold walls to talk to. I felt very lonely.

The lack of understanding and miscommunication had hugely impacted my relationship with my mother. I absolutely resented the way she monopolized me doing things I really do not like. For this, I later on did everything I could to fight against her. Our relationship was approaching icy cold.

Resentments . . . .

For days, I was not well emotionally. Sometimes I wonder how I survived those days. When I was struggling with school works and with classmates at school, I had no one to turn to but the cold bricks in the house. I did not know what or how to discuss with classmates with my schoolings. I remember when my mother called me in those days, she never asked me how I was, but how I scored academically. Ironically, if I was not well both emotionally or physically, how would I be able to score well? I was really not well, and I was told by my brother to keep my feelings to myself so I did not make my parents worry. Life is hard, and it gets harder when there is no one to share your thoughts with.

CHAPTER 6

The Myths About Straight–A Students

Buddha said: All sentient being is the nature of light,
there is no worry.

Buddhism advocates equality in life. There is no birth or death, but it is just the natural being This topic is an in-depth one and takes a lot of thinking and discussion. Well, if I would be able to put that into perspective, then scoring high at schooling perhaps is something that we can correlate.

I scored above average academically, but never really scored at the very top. Being a perfectionist, I had always yearned to score at the top of the class when I was little. However it was never the case. I might occasionally score a bit higher, but was never at the top. I was able to get through my schoolings with sufficient scores. In fact, as English was not my first language, I actually scored poorly in English during my high school years. I guess in those days when you have too many personal issues, your intellectual side would be pretty blocked and dysfunctional. Learning a new language was not hard for me, but it was the reality side of life that actually struck me the most.

Over the years, I came to accept who I am. I was never able to TOP the class. There are only certain things you can achieve and obtain, but others are simply unattainable. It is like the fact that fish will never be able to fly (except flying fish which only fly temporarily above water), and it will be hard for birds to learn to swim underwater like fish (except seagulls which will only float above water but never under).

There are always questions that I often ask all these years:

If you are not a straight-A student, how can you expect your child to be one?

If everyone scores straight-A's, then who are there to score B's or C's?

Who can guarantee that straight-A students will have secure jobs in the future?

As a child, I had always been a good student. I scored above 90% for most of my academic results in both primary school and junior high schools when I used to live in Taiwan. However, after I moved to Australia in my teenage years, things changed. The language barrier became the major obstacle for me. Furthermore, I had other issues to sort out. Back in Taiwan, I have always had my parents doing all the chores, and it would not be exaggerating if I said I was spoon-fed in Taiwan during schooling. However, living in Sydney, I needed to learn how to look after myself, and it was quite challenging.

One friend of mine was a straight-A student. She even got a scholarship throughout her university years. Everything went so well for her. Of course she worked extremely hard to score so high academically. Now, she is more than well paid and got to travel around the whole globe simply because she works hard, and she has the right mindset to do so. Guess what? Both of her parents were straight-A students! There must be a linkage between the parents and children in terms of their intellectual abilities.

When I was younger (and still to this date), my father always made comparison between me and her. It used to upset me to a great extent. I was not so willing not to talk to her (my friend) and her father! They always bragged about how her great achievements! Of course their parents are proud of her! There is no doubt about that, but do you know what the problem is? I am not her, I am simply my parents' kid, and I will never be the same way that my friend is. My background is totally different from hers and I got my genes from you, my beloved parents, but not from the straight-A girl's parents! Now I am a lot more mature and am able to stand outside of the box, think, and talk clearly. I was able to defend myself against my father's accusation that I was not willing to be competitive to my next door neighbor.

She may have all the talent she has, but we simply are two different individuals. It all boils down to the fact that you have to accept who you really are, and not feel inferior if you have not achieved as highly as your peers. It was a hard lesson I learned throughout my life. I learned to be my own guidance and constant told myself that not achieving something does not mean that you are any lower than anyone else. That was a lesson to be kind to myself. There is absolutely no point to beat yourself up like that, to tell yourself that you are a failure, or even to allow your loved ones to sabotage your pride like that. It is simply detrimental to be beaten up like that.

To a very proud person like myself, harmful words look like: Look at xxx, she has made xxx amount of money, how about YOU? She has gone through university without having to ask money from her parents, WHAT about YOU? For years, those words were like swords sliding into my heart; it was unbearable. For years, I learned to tell myself that I am simply not her, and that we have very different backgrounds. Life is a journey, and it is not a sports game in which you constantly need to compare yourself to others, or score higher than others. It is simply a pathway and we all have different routes to head to. Sometimes we collide, and sometimes we separate into different pathways. *The most important thing is myself,* I constantly reminded myself. If there is anyone you should compete with, it is you who you need to conquer, not ANYONE else.

Now I learn to appreciate others' success and hopefully I can grasp any life experience from them. It is my very interest to share their success and to be happy for them. I learned to be very generous with my words and appraisal. The positive words are great bridging over ice-breaking when you try to raise a conversation. If there are personal stories and insights I can learn from others, why not? If it is only a couple of positive words I need to spare and it might lead to an insightful and meaningful conversation, why not? People nowadays have gone cold and it can be quite hard to break the ice. I now treasure my sentimental nature as a gift. It is this gift that I learn from my life that has connected me with all the wonderful friends I have encountered, and they are happy to share their life stories that have made abundance in my life. I appreciate that.

I admire straight-A students. They work extremely hard to maintain their high-standard work. I have noticed that most of them have been able to achieve highly in a corporate world later on in their lives. They were trained at young ages to achieve high scores, hence later on they will be aiming for high KPIs, and all the rest of scores that account for high ranks in the company. This is possibility the main reason parents regard academic scores highly for their children; it encapsulates the idea that the higher score you get, the higher possibility with which your career pathway is paved.

The straight-A students' high self-esteem inspire me. They can endure long working hours and sometimes can be too nerdy to start a conversation with. Yes, that is possibly the main reason Asian parents will also educate their kids to aim for high scores at school.

However, not every single person can achieve high academically. There will always be people who are at mediocrity and lower levels. There are people who are simply not good at academic works! There is REALLY nothing wrong with that. This does not mean that they will never achieve somewhere else, right? This world is filled with diversity and if we are all trained to achieve the highest scores, then what fun would we have to have in this world? A world filled with identical cloned people from the most advanced genetic cloning? That would be the empirical world of the future world when the human technology has advanced so much, and it would become so boring!

Everyone has a different pathway in life, and every single human being is unique. Everyone has a different capacity in life to reach.

Everyone has different talents specifically. Sometimes one cannot reinforce one thing to another.

It is like a bird will never know how to swim under water, and a fish can never learn how to fly. Flying fish can temporarily fly over water for a few seconds, but never really have the ability to fly. The seagull can float above water briefly, but they will never be able to dive into deep water.

My mother later on realized there is no point pushing me to be someone I am not. She loves who I am, and that is the most important thing. She just wants me to be happy. This is called unconditional love. The feeling of being understood meant a lot to me. Without some unnecessary expectation, I was able to live freely with my soul and soar above what I want to achieve. I searched for the meaning of my life, for what I really wanted instead of what my parents or my mother expects me to be. There is nothing worse than living under someone else's shadow, or to live under someone's dreams when they are not yours.

A Side Story—A Proud Mother

To go side tracked a bit, let me share a story with you.

This is a mother I encountered somewhere. She is an extremely proud mother of her daughter. I really don't understand why some mothers love bragging about their daughters. Their ideas about their daughters can be quite biased sometimes.

There was this lady who had a daughter of my age. Every time I saw her in social events, she always liked to mention her daughter. She enjoyed talking about her daughter TO ME immensely. I suppose I reminded her of her daughter?

People can be quite competitive in the Asian community. This lady seemed like one of them. The first time she saw me, she made a huge point about how pretty her daughter is . . . "My daughter is extremely pretty. She has loads of guys chasing after her!" She told me.

She must have repeated herself a couple of times before I could stop her. In fact there was nothing I could do to stop her. She was quite indulged in her own thoughts of her daughter's beauty. I spent the next thirty minutes allowing her to blow my ears with her daughter's glamour without even seeing the daughter in my whole entire life. It was not until I later saw her daughter in real life that I realized her daughter looked IDENTICAL to her, just younger! They even dressed so much alike!

I murmured to myself, "Such a waste of my thirty minutes being ear-blown by her!" I really should have told the mother,

"Firstly I am not a gay, I am not interested in your daughter.

Secondly, I am not a man, so I will not chase your daughter.

Thirdly, even if I am either a gay or a man, I will not even go close to your daughter! To have a mother-in-law like you will really take me to HEAVEN!"

This lady continued her mission of showing off her daughter. The second time I met her in the public, she mentioned to me that she was getting her daughter a BMW car! The third time I saw her, she was getting the daughter a mansion in a luxury district! Thank my merciful Buddha that I never had to meet her the fourth time, otherwise I think she would have come back and told me that she was getting her daughter a helicopter?!

Somebody just never knows where and how to put a break on the pedal . . . .

CHAPTER 7

The Surgery, Racial Discrimination?

I believe the ultimate source of blessing is within us.
A good motivation and honesty brings self-confidence,
which attracts the trust and respect of others.
~Julia Ho

I did not have too much luck in my university years. In fact, I think I was even lucky to get into university doing pharmacy. My academic results in my university years were not great, except for math, my easiest subject. The math we did in the first year of university was the expansion of the four units maths we did in high school. I guess being good at plotting all the formulae and having a bit of logic helps. That is the beauty of math—you do not need to memorize too much, but having the right logic is the magical way to get you through the mathematical realm.

Other than that, the chemistry really shocked me in a pathetic way—long hours of working out how these biomedical formulae and interactions confused me. I am really not good at tackling those biomedical matters.

In my university years, I was still dealing with my resentment at my experience and also at my mother's matriarchal behaviour. Also on a personal level, I had a very bad relationship, a detrimental one. Even

42

when he was almost out of my life by moving overseas, my drama and endless unhappiness did not end there. All my close friends had moved overseas in my first or second year of university. It made my social life even harder. I was constantly yearning for the ones who had moved overseas and forgot those I had beside me as friends. I guess that is when all the insecurity kicked in. I had trouble focusing on what I was doing, including my university studies.

One day I was working at the laboratory trying to work out the exact concentration of the solution as part of pharmaceutical curriculum, and a major accident happened. I used a pipette to suck out the solution from the tube, and accidentally the pipette broke from the middle and I stabbed myself with the broken sharp pipette. I saw my own blood splashing through the floor of the laboratory. I was terrified, petrified and shocked. The pain was unbearable and excruciating. Both physical pain and emotional shock were so intense that moment that I could immediately faint. However, my inner voice told me that I needed to be very calm not to faint or hit myself against any sharp ends in the laboratory to add any extra drama on top of what had just happened. I told myself that I could only collapse when someone came and rescued me. There were a few seconds of silence and I quickly shouted out to the rest of the class. I remember I cried it out the loudest I could with my faint voice, *Help!* Finally I did draw someone's attention and later on I landed on someone's hand and collapsed.

The next second I could hear someone calling me, "Julia. Julia." Since I was in a state of shock and devastation, all I could see was the image of black and white. I was unable to respond to whoever was calling me. I was practically in semi-coma. I could vaguely remember someone had the emergency knowledge with this sort of incident to have my hands and arms elevated above my heart so I would not over bleed. They tried to stop the bleeding and ensure my left hand and arm were in the elevated level so no excessive bleeding occurred.

The laboratory was located on the second floor and there was more than one person who assisted me to reach the ground level. I seriously do not recall how I reached the ground level; maybe someone held me in his arms and took me straight down. I do not recall myself walking down at all.

Finally I was taken to the GP in the university campus and was treated as an emergency. By this stage my injured left index finger was very well wrapped up by the medical stuff, and the bleeding had stopped. I was kept in the medical practice to wait for further arrangement from the doctor. In the meantime, the doctor had advised me to keep my arm and finger raised above my heart level to avoid bleeding.

The GP doctor carefully examined my finger and asked me with regards to the sensation. The preliminary diagnosis was that I had cut the nerve of my index finger. I was later on transported to the hospital by the university ambulance. It really felt like a cab ride and the driver was a very nice man. On the way to the hospital, the driver did his best to cheer me up. There is nothing more elevating when someone shares and gives a bit of comfort and positive words whilst you are in pain.

When I reached the hospital, I was taken to the sick bed to rest and there was another waiting game. Finally they had the finger specialist come and examine me, and decided that my injury was not life-threatening, and the surgery would partake the next day.

Waiting at the hospital sick bed was no fun. I was scared. I have never been into a hospital bed like that, and it was scary to be there alone. My mobile phone had run out of battery at that point. I was practically sobbing. The nurse who was looking after me came and checked on me, and I told her that I was in pain, and I needed to make phone calls to my friend or my mother. Thankfully my mother was in Sydney. Otherwise I would have had no one to help me with normal routine life after being discharged from the hospital. I never knew that crying made a huge impact on this hospitalization incident. People did notice me when I was trying to make a remark. The nurse quickly realized how much pain I was and how desperately I needed to make a phone call to my friend.

I rang a very good friend of mine from high school, Eva. She is from HK and lives in the neighbourhood. She used to teach me Cantonese pronunciation word by word so that later on I was able to speak the language properly.

The minute Eva answered my call, she told me that she had just finished working and was very tired, meaning to tell me that if I needed to talk, we would have to do it some other time. Well, I was in the hospital, I told Eva. I had injured my finger and had been sent to emergency. Eva quickly realized the emergency and she offered to go and collect my mother from my house to bring her to the hospital to see me. They also managed to find my car in the university campus and drove it home later on.

When Eva came with my mother and her friend, my mother practically cried. She did not know what to do. Neither did I. Eva was good at comforting my mother with a huge smile. I remember faintly thanking her for taking my mother to the hospital. It was at that moment that I realized how important it is to have an honourable friend like Eva, someone who will always be standing beside you to cherish in your joy and share your pain with you.

My mother was vey devastated later on to learn that the hospital would not allow any family members to stay overnight in the hospital. She had to go home that night and the surgery would take place the next morning. She was initially planning to hide underneath my bed, but eventually gave up. She came and visited the next day to be there with me for the surgery.

It was a huge ward in which I was staying. There was not anybody beside me the day I was admitted to the hospital. I had a phone and a television all by myself, with the rest of the empty beds besides me. It was sort of good to be left alone so I was not disturbed at all.

The surgery took more than eight hours when they told my mother initially it would take somewhere between three and four hours. The finger injured was my left index finger. They did a microsurgery to my hand to stitch up the injuries of the nerves that were damaged by the pipette. I had twelve stitches at the end after being repairing with a micro-surgical procedure.

Before the surgery, I remember the anaesthetic doctor asking me questions to ensure I knew what was going on as part of the anaesthetic procedure. There were few questions he had to ask before

I was knocked out. I remember he told me, "Julia, the minute you are injected with the anaesthetics, you will just go into sleep." Ha! I was knocked out straight after that moment. I sort of woke up whilst the surgeons were conducting the surgery, and then I went back into a coma again, but somehow I overheard the doctors talking. I am presuming they were doing something very serious to my hand!

After the surgery was completed I was sent to the recovery. The doctors had told my mother the surgery was a success. The minute I saw my mother, she was seemingly anxious about what had been happening in the surgery room. Well, it took a lot longer than what she was told. Her anxious, long face was memorable to me. People always yearn for hopes and positive outcomes, and so did my mother. Someone was very creative to tell my mother to make 1,000 origami stars; it would enhance your opportunity to make a wish. So she did. In the following three days of staying in the hospital, she was at my bedside folding all these origami stars from recycling papers and then at the completion of 1,000 stars, she made a wish. Well, a wishful thought that I will eventually recuperate well from this injury.

Miraculously I did recover well from this injury. It has been more than fifteen years since that accident, and the scar was almost unnoticeable. BIG thanks to my mother! The strength of willpower is immensely strong. Later on when I quarrelled with my mother and complained to my friend, Eva, my very truly friend had pointed out my mother's love to me when she was looking after me throughout the process of the surgery, including her sincerity of making a wish with 1,000 origami stars, showing me that I should allow some space to think it through. Eva was right. Regardless of how differently I think than my mother, how resentful I felt towards my mother, that will never alter the motherly love. Of course, there is a huge amount of contradictory and complex feelings involved.

That night my mother rang me as soon as she reached home. She was sobbing over the phone, and yet I was the one who was in pain! She asked me over the phone, "Are you in pain?" As much as I was suffering, I had to lie to her that it was bearable and okay.

I said to her, "I am okay, Mom, do not worry about me." In fact, I was in excruciating pain. As soon as I hung up the phone, I started crying. I was the one who was suffering physical pain and I was the one who had to comfort my beloved mother! Thankfully I had a good night's sleep at the hospital which made my hospitalized days better and the whole process of recuperation progressed.

My hospital days were not too bad except for the pain. After the surgery I was kept in the hospital for another three days just to make sure the wound was healing properly before I was sent home. Luckily the ward I stayed in was practically empty in the first two days of my stay. I was not disturbed at all. I had a huge TV in front of me with a remote control handy at my bedside. I also had a direct line all to myself in case someone rang. I was allowed to make endless phone calls to any landlines, so I made the best out of it. I rang my friends to kill my boredom.

The pain and the shock from the incident had a huge impact on my appetite. I was unable to eat. The food that was provided at the hospital went mostly to my mother. I could only have a few bites and then could not eat any further. My mother would come and stay with me at my bedside in the morning and then go home according to the hospital rule. They did not allow any carers or relatives to stay overnight in the hospital. In the morning when my mother came, she would bring food from home, freshly cooked so in case I do not favour the food in the hospital, at least I had something to fall back on.

At this instant I am writing this, I still feel a bit emotional at my mother's unspoken words of love. She would always be there staying beside me, folding origami stars by my side; each fold represented her love, the unspoken words. Now I wonder if she was ever to express more of her words of love, just a little bit more than she could. Perhaps if she was able to tell me more of her feelings, I would be more understanding and later on have less resentment towards her.

After three days we were sent home. My friend came over and collected us. We were all set to go. According to the physiologist, since my bones were a lot more flexible than average, it would take twelve weeks to recover instead of eight weeks. In the long run it is good; since my bones showed a lot more flexibility than most people, the recuperating outcome seems promising, but with the addition of four weeks with the cast on. They had my casted cemented to ensure the fixation of the bones during recovery. I had to also go to physiotherapy according to the remedial regime, depending on how I was recuperating. I was asked to go back to my specialist on a regular basis so they could check on my wound healing process.

Since I was very shocked by the incident, my appetite was heavily affected. I was unable to eat. I could still remember my mother making a whole pot of fried rice and I could only have a few bites and that was it. I could not bear to see any knives. So I distanced myself from all the sharpening tools, knives especially. I was very petrified by the incident. Emotionally, I was shocked.

There was a whole team of the surgeons who worked together on my finger. The chief surgeon supervised the surgeons who did the surgery on me, and the rest of the team were there observing the whole process. They often had discussions on the prognosis of the patients, so when I did go back for assessment and further check up, I could basically go to any of them. It seems that they see the patients in the rotation basis. Once I got to be seen by the Chief, once I got to be seen by the other doctor, and most of the time I was seen by the doctor who operated on me.

I vaguely remember the doctor who operated on me had a first name of Steve. He was very proud of my outcome. I am his proud patient. Everything went so well. Fifteen years ago when they did the micro-surgery to stitch up the nerves, I am sure the technology was not as advanced as it is today. Presumably they were still quite new? I am not sure. All I knew was that every time I went back to the doctors to be seen, they all were so proud of me. I was doing very well. In addition to the happy outcome, all the doctors recognized me as the "crying patient." Well, I was quite emotional and afraid to go through that procedure. It was the very first time in my memory I'd ever been admitted to the hospital for three days.

"So you are the good patient, also the crying one?" the doctors asked me with recognition. I really don't know if I should be proud of my way to make the gesture or what? But I certainly did make a huge impression amongst the surgeons.

The physiotherapist, Jackie, was a very patient person. In the initial stage of physiotherapy, I had to go twice a week. The physiotherapist would have a huge bowl of warm water for me to soak in for approximately ten minutes so the scar would soften, then she would carefully remove the old dead skin. According to Jackie, this whole process was to remove the dead skin and enhance the growth of new skins.

Immediately after the surgery, my finger was swollen like a huge sausage. The stitches were still there and it was very painful to move or even wiggle. After the stitches were removed, I was instructed to move my fingers slowly. At first, I did not move my index finger as I was instructed. I can still clearly remember Jackie scolding at me, saying, "Julia, would you like your finger kinky like this without too much movement in ten years' time?" I will always remember her stern look on her face. Of course my answer to her was "NO." That day I returned home being a goodie-goodie; I went home following the instructions I was told. When she asked me to do ten folding movements, I would do ten, no more and no less. I was a very obedient and diligent patient.

Despite all the painful experiences, I always knew this whole thing would turn out to be OKAY. I had faith in myself that my injured finger will be fine. It turned out to be quite true. Fifteen years later, my left index finger turned out to be FINE. If I had not mentioned that I have an injury in my finger to anyone, no one would notice. The injury did not affect my movement, nor had there any apparent signs, except a huge scar left from the twelve stitches. If there is any chance I could go back and thank the surgeons again, I would. They really did an extremely good job, as initially identified.

It was towards the end of the year when the final exam came through. I was still not catching up well with my studies. Since I was only doing very few subjects that year (I repeated the first year a second time), I had more time to recuperate properly. It was approaching final exams and the chief surgeon suggested going to the university to ask for extend time for my exams. As pointed out by the surgeon, the pain would somewhat affect my performance, hence I needed more time to do my exam. Even though I am right-handed, and my injured finger was my left index finger, technically my writing would not be affected. However the pain should still be factored in, according to the Chief surgeon.

I went through all these troubles to find the right contact of doctors for arranging an extension of my exam time. As part of this process, all the professors for the subjects I was studying got to know me. Well, part of it was because my name was pretty straightforward to remember, Julia Ho.

Eventually I did find the right contact doctor responsible to assess this. To my amazement, this doctor refused to give me any extension right to my face. He said straight away with his cold tongue, "I don't think you need any extension of the exam, since you are right handed."

I said to him, "But MY doctor told me I would still go through some certain degree of pain, so I should be granted a longer time for the exam."

He swayed his head and you could see his face expression saying, "I am done here, so get out of my office". His reluctance really struck me. I was infuriated and frustrated. I said to him, "You do not know how painful it is!" Well, I was obviously challenging his authority and his speciality by saying that!

And his response was a very surprising answer: "You don't know what I went through with my life." That sounds absolutely ridiculous. I ran out of the door with my cast on, and in tears.

I quickly ran to my surgeon's clinic without even asking for an appointment. The surgeon's team took turns seeing their patients. The day I went back, I was lucky to see my own surgeon, Steve. He was very surprised to see me.

"We don't expect to see you here today. What can we do for you, Julia?"

With my famous tearful look, I started explaining what was going on when I went to see the local GP in the university. "The GP would not give me more time for my exam!" I cried.

"Bureaucratic!" Steve was very angry the instant when I told him the story. Perhaps my crying strategy also worked? He took his writing pad straight out of the drawer and wrote whatever was necessary. I think my face was still filled with tears when I stared at him.

"So who do I ask for?" I asked.

"Me!" he answered. Dr. Steve quickly jotted down ALL his contact details and made sure the contact details were clearly stated. "If he needs to talk to anyone, this is my number. Ask him to call ME!" he said with an assertive attitude.

Following that, I went straight back to the University Clinic. As soon as I saw the university GP, I said to him, "My doctor wants me to hand this over to you!" The doctor had the most confused look on his face. I knew I was winning; I was almost laughing from my heart. I turned away from the GP and was ready to leave. Then I turned back and reminded him, "by the way, my doctor's contact details are HERE" I pointed out the contact details to him and made sure he got the message. So off I went with a grin in both my face and heart. I smiled.

Eventually I did get my extension for the exam, but that did not really help my result. I still failed; I was simply not studying properly. Sometime later I went back to the surgeon's for my follow-up check-up. I had a chance to talk to the Chief, and had brief words with the GP from the university. I said to the Chief, "That GP doctor was racist!"

The Chief was very cautious and took me aside and told me in a low tone, "Julia, racist is a very strong word. You'd better be careful what you are talking about! The GP doctor just has a very different opinion on what we were talking about. But he did eventually agree to grant you more time for the exam!"

Ha! *I won*, I told myself. I am a very assertive person, a strong-minded person who will not allow people to walk over me. I will definitely speak out if the time allows. I did, and I will, and I will always do.

CHAPTER 8
The Rebellious Julia

If you realized how powerful your thoughts are,
you would never think a negative thought.
~Peace Pilgrim

Sometimes people learn things in the hard way. I did.

Sometimes people allow their negative emotions take control of their life. I did.

Sometimes the negative thoughts prevail and people end up trapped in those faulty situations created by one-self. I did.

Sometimes greed and desires drive you to endless torments. I did.

At the age of early twenty, I realized I was almost spending all my life fighting over my mother. I was very unhappy. The negative emotions took over my life. Deep inside, I knew I needed help. I was talking to one of my auntie's friends when I made that realization.

"Maybe you were doing this to get your mother's attention?" she asked me.

"Yes". The minute she pointed that out, I burst into tears.

All my life, I thought I was never noticed or heard by my mother. Unfortunately I used the very poor tactics to grab my mother's attention. At a young age, I behaved well to make myself comfortable with my mother. I loved to make my mother proud of me, making myself presentable when she took me around. I was a goodie-goodie, a very well-behaved student, with good grades and good manners, and I worked myself hard to ensure all the criteria of a good daughter was met. I was also driven by my desire to be noticed and loved, and my lack of security, my not being sure if I had made any mistakes, and my fear that I would fail my mother.

While still being a good student, I started showing my rebellious side. This was the emotional side of myself that was not satisfied. In simple words, I tried every angle to ensure that I had my mother's attention. I must admit that I am an attention seeker. This arose from my lack of security and my need to be noticed.

In primary school, I was a well-behaved student. I got good grades, had my homework handed in on time . . . all the positive attributes of a good student. However, I needed to look after myself after school starting when I was only in the first grade. I learned to be quite independent when I was as young as seven or eight. I needed to ensure I had the key to go home and made sure I was safe.

I felt that I was simply too young to start that process, to be independent! It was that resentment that initiated the rebellious behaviour. The mixed feelings of resentments, lack of security, and endless questions to why I could NOT see my mother after school persisted. When you start slicing those very intricate emotions, you start realizing that questions of *why* and *how* can get quite complicated as you grow up. Those negative thoughts could eventuate into faulty behaviours even though I may have presented as a good student externally. It is like a beautiful apple with a rotten inside. My resentment and lack of security made me a rebellious person later on, and all of that was targeted at my mother. Revenge would probably be too strong to describe it—or should I say emotional blackmailing?

When you yearn for something that you truly desire, you would do anything for it. But what if you are yearning for attention from your own mother? What would you do?

For me, the worst part was that it exploded in a very negative way. I began to do everything to grab her attention from every single angle I could.

Since I was little, I was even shoplifting from the shop. I wanted to have the things I desired but I knew my mother would never agree to purchase them for me. Thankfully it was only a process in life and soon I rectified that bad habit. I once read in a book that shoplifting is actually a very common bad habit when people are growing up. There must be a rationale behind it, though. Now when I think back to those days of shoplifting I realize that my desire was not being fulfilled, and that feeling of lacking was what prompted my stealing.

In my junior high school, my teacher was a very strict one. She had taught us to achieve as much as we could to get good grades, hence going on to good high schools and good universities, going on to get a good job, etc.

When you are a rebel, you are a rebel from the inside. I love challenges. I love seeing things from a very different angle. I love seeing things from outside of the box. When I saw my teacher forcing us to work so hard academically—and she used every modality to ensure we sat in front of the desk for long hours to achieve academic results—my rebellious nature was evoked. I was really unhappy, and I did not think that rigorous academic study was the only way to success. I challenged my teacher.

In our junior high school years, we were supposed to hand in a diary to the teacher as a daily report. Our teacher used her own power to have her daughter in our class, and her daughter seemed to be performing well all the time. It appeared to us that this was an unfair situation and something fishy was going on. I always wrote in my diary, subtly criticising her way of supervising us. I wrote about how I thought it was not necessary for us to stay long hours after school hours, ie: after 5:00 pm. I questioned why her daughter always got almost 100% for her quiz, asking if there was some sort of cheating going on in the background or if she was simply really smart. Such a questioning tone was in my dairy. Of course my teacher could study my hostile feelings towards her, but there was nothing she could to do me; I was a GOOD student. You see, when you feel that you are magically empowered, then you can use that magic power to sabotage people's feelings. I was that cheeky!

My best friend Noriko was leaving for Japan by the first semester of year eight. She had to go and learn Japanese after school, therefore she was unable to stay after school with the rest of the class. Everyone, including myself, envied her for being able to leave early. Our teacher started treating her awkwardly and considered her leaving early to be a lack of class participation. Well, she had to learn Japanese; she was heading to Japan! Teacher Jing was giving her negative comments about how she performed badly, and sort of commented that I should not mingle with her since she was considered a "bad" student, and I was considered a "good" student.

It was quite terrible to be labelled as a "good" or "bad" student—either way it was not healthy. The "good" label on a student means that she was somehow superior to the others because she was performing well academically. This sort of ego does not get you anywhere. Because no one is perfect, being academically well-achieved does not guarantee you anything. It probably adds a higher possibility of a successful career path, but it's not a 100% guarantee.

On the other hand, a student labelled as being a "bad" student does not necessary mean that she will not do any better in other respects of life. Maybe she does not fit into the current mainstream education system, but that does not mean she is incapable of performing other things well.

Noriko was a classic example of this. She did not fit into the academic system in Taiwan. She could not take the highly pressured academic system in Taiwan, and the labelling was too much for her. Being pressurized by heavy schooling did not push her to achieve well in the local education system in Taiwan, but that does not necessarily mean she had no chance of achieving academic results! Later on she had the chance to pursue her academic realm in the United States, and she still did complete her Bachelor's Degree. She took the liberty in her mindset to ensure she could finish a university degree.

As Ms. Jing's attitude towards Noriko was getting worse, Noriko was feeling unjust. Noriko's sister wrote a letter to the education system reporting Ms. Jing. In a way, Ms. Jing's attitude could have been treated from a legal approach. In those days a lot of teachers were holding cramming school after school hours. It served as a secondary job on top of the teachers' daily jobs. The money they made out of it would be quite paramount. Students' parents would be happy and honoured to send their kids to those cram schools as they were treated special. The teachers were coaching students either after school hours or on the weekends, so the students were able to receive supplementary study guides. However it was illegal for the teacher to do so after school hours. It was in breach of the law, as they might favour the students who were going to the cram schools over the ones who did not go. So to play it safe, it was important for the teachers to select the students carefully, so such after-school services were not reported.

Ms. Jing had a school held after school hours. Noriko was placed in the cram school in the first year as requested by Noriko's mother. Because I was close to Noriko, I got to know all the proceedings throughout the whole process. Personally, I was very much against Ms. Jing's stringent way of pushing academic results, and I was on Noriko's side to ensure she was doing okay. It was just a process to prove to yourself that you were on the justified side instead of being unfairly treated. I was acting as a bridge to pass on messages of what was said by each side, but I never actually got involved. Ms. Jing and Noriko both called me often to update me on the current situation. I never knew how it eventuated, but I had my share of clearly expressing my thoughts towards Ms. Jing. I told Ms. Jing what I thought was right without fear of whether or not it would offend her. I was very assertive of what I thought and was not afraid of expressing myself.

At the age of thirteen, my rebel side started showing. Even when I was a good student performing well, I was not one of those who just nodded their heads all the time. I was not afraid of telling people what I thought was right, even it meant challenging the higher authority at the time, my teacher.

After I came to Australia at the age of fourteen my mother's plotting did not satisfy me. I was mostly left alone in the house during my teenage years, and I had no one to share in such drama but myself. I became a loner and I thought that it might be easier to deal with things on my own. I tried to take others' suggestions to make things work. Unfortunately a lot of those suggestions did not serve me right. Firstly, they were not the people who got involved in my situation. Secondly they were only on-lookers. They were not involved. Well, okay, okay, they were simply not involved in my situation; why bother asking their opinions?

Starting in the late high school years, I became quite rebellious. I needed to grab my mother's attention. I needed to show her who I was, what I could do.

I was speaking words against her will. I was fighting against her and would not obey what I was told. Worst of all, I was no longer able to perform well academically. I had lost my ability to study well. My brain was so full of negativity that I was not thinking straight.

Being rebellious, spending noticeable amounts of money, going out late at night and coming home late . . . I did everything I could to get her attention. On the other hand, I was avoiding her as much as I could. The days we were living together, she was either visiting me in Sydney, or after I had moved back to Taiwan I just tried to do anything to get myself out of her face. I did not want to see her. I would wake up later than her or I would come home late so that by the time I arrived home, she had already gone to sleep.

It was my way to show my resentment, but if you ask me whether I was happy to do so? I can tell you the truth: Absolutely NOT. I was not happy. I had used every single cell of my body to defend myself against her. That had consumed a tremendous amount of energy, and it was also exhausting. It was also a very negative way to show how much I truly needed her attention. At some point I communicated with my mother ONLY if necessary, and only when I needed money or her help. It was quite selfish to say so, but that was so true.

My relationship with my mother at the time was quite bad, unpleasant, and negative. However, neither of us knew what was going wrong. We were simply not communicating. They say that to love is to hate. This might be a perfect answer for it. We love each other very much, but something was very wrong. Very, very wrong.

CHAPTER 9

Tzu Chi Buddhist Foundation

However many holy words you read,
however many you speak,
what good will they do you
if you do not act on upon them?
~Buddha

Remember I included the footprint quote earlier in this book? I think the guardian angels must have presented themselves in various different forms. I was introduced to the Tzu Chi Buddhist Foundation in the last two years of my first stay in Sydney. It is an absolute turning point in both my life and in my mother's life. Buddha's wisdom was taught and passed to my dearest mother. It is magical.

With Master Cheng Yen's words to express Buddha's wisdom, she taught us that good luck and fortune does not come from simply praying, but also action. The praying action is the essence of faith and belief, but more importantly, it is how and what you have put into action. That is the very crucial part of correct Buddhism belief.

In the years of bad patches, I went to counselling at the University of Sydney. The counsellor guided me to a way to think logically. With the rest of the free time, I had a chance to associate with the

Tzu Chi Buddhist Foundation. It was at this time that I met Mother Lin. ("Mother" is the Chinese version of calling someone who is your senior; placing either "Father" or "Mother" in front of the surname shows respect.)

I met Mother Lin when I was in a pretty bad shape. I was quite skinny at the time. I hardly ate because I could not. The mental stress had been so bad that was preventing me from eating properly. In those times I could only eat one meal a day, and I lived on a lollipop in the morning to provide sugar to my body. It feels like at some point I probably only had bone left in me. I was also looking quite frail. Things were not looking good. I did not know what to do, because nothing seemed to be working—my university work was a struggle, my relationship with my mother was deteriorating, I didn't have many friends, and most importantly, I simply could not face any more daily responsibilities on my own anymore. I had lost strength and had no faith in my own abilities.

Mother Lin came to me as a guardian angel to introduce me to the wisdom of Buddha. Her smile was angelic. As a member of the Tzu Chi Buddhist Foundation, she brought both Buddha and Master Cheng Yen's wisdom to the lives of my mother and I. I can still remember Mother Lin's lovely smile and the warmth of her palm when she held my hand—at the time my mother had refused to talk to me.

I believe that one's biggest challenge in life is to challenge yourself and to confront your own innermost demon, to be willing to change for betterment, to make recognition of your own good and bad. My mother found the wisdom through Buddha's words. Because she changed, it provided the pathway for me to learn from Buddha's teaching as well.

The three No's in the world.

> *There is no one in this world I don't forgive.*
> *There is on one in this world I don't love.*
> *There is no one in this world I don't trust.*

One has to step out of her own world and see the other end of the world. In Tzu Chi's community work, my mother did just this. Before my mother was heavily involved with the charity activities, she was an ordinary woman whose primary focus was on the family, and on the family business which was heavily caught up with the family finances. When you look at things too closely, sometimes you lose perspective; you do not fully grasp the whole picture. Hence it is good to step aside for a moment. Then you may come back with a whole different idea. Tzu Chi charity activities provide the platform for this.

The primary teaching of the founder of the Tzu Chi Buddhist Foundation, Master Cheng Yen, is to put words into action instead of only chanting Buddhist words. She emphasises that as Buddhists we are obliged to take actions to help others, based on Buddha's wisdom. However helping others requires a lot of knowledge and the establishment of boundaries. The learning process should be life-long, as it is never-ending.

The essence of the Tzu Chi Buddhist Foundation consists of four missions including Charity, Medicine, Education, and Culture. Furthermore, considering ongoing efforts in Bone Marrow Donation, Environmental Protection, Community Volunteerism, and International Relief, these eight concurrent campaigns are collectively known as "Tzu Chi's Eight footprints." It depends on how you were first approached, but people get involved with all sorts of activities, or at least most of them.

My mother first got involved with the study group for reading. There are a lot of books on the Tzu Chi. Some of them are written by Master Cheng Yen, and some of them are the life stories shared amongst the sisters and brothers. When my mother was here in Sydney, they were a lot of study groups in the community when people share their stories and feelings throughout the words of learning. In the study group, people gather together on a regular basis and appoint a certain book to read. People are also assigned certain questions to share for the next session. Sharing in front of other people serve a few purposes, including self-reflection and repentance.

When you have approached a bottleneck in life, perhaps it is time to utilize a different approach in life; perhaps it is time for you to change. It is time to turn back to Buddha's wisdom. Reading is actually a different form of meditation when people gather together to share thoughts. Different people's ideas spark with each other to raise thought and learning to a different level.

In Master Cheng Yen's teaching, one should treat your children like others' children. This is to teach you to treat your own child lightly and without too much expectation, to allow your child to have a bit of space. This teaches the parents not to take burdens upon themselves worrying their children because worrying does not help, and it will only increase tension between the parents and kids. So getting involved with Tzu Chi's activities is a great opportunity to divert focus when someone is primarily focusing on their families. It is time to go and help others who are suffering.

My mother became a very dedicated member of the study group. After we all went back to Taiwan, she found herself a study group held every Wednesday. Everyone gathers together studying books. It is not a conventional study group where people only study books; the leader was quite creative to modulate activities involved. In the study group, people share thoughts, people are trained to talk in front of others and then in the public, and people are trained to organize public activities.

In the space of fifteen years, my mother grew from a person who was so afraid of microphones to a woman who now speaks in front of 400 to 500 people. It is an amazing growth process throughout that space of time.

When I went back to Taiwan I struggled heavily with work during the first few years. I went back to work with my mother for a few months when I was heavily depressed. She took me in so that she knew I was okay. One day she was on her way to her study group and sent me off home, but I begged to go with her. I did not want to go home alone. My mother suddenly realized that I could go and study with her.

The pair of us went to the study group for at least three years together. In the space of three years of time, my mother and I bonded together again. We learned to hold hands together.

The greatest change my mother has undergone throughout the learning process in the Tzu Chi charity group is in the fact that she is no longer narrow-minded. She is no longer locked up in her own world judging people by their monetary statuses. She opened her heart and arms to reach out for the ones who are in need. She filled others with smiles, and so the laughter comes back to her. Her perspective of money has changed in the process of getting involved with the charity.

Perhaps it is sensible for me to briefly introduce the primary essence of the Tzu Chi Buddhist Foundation. The Tzu Chi Foundation has been very transparent with the funds it has raised and in how they are managed. The cost of running the Tzu Chi Foundation is raised by the masters working, themselves. They grow plants in the fields to be self-sufficient. They make all sorts of things including different flavours of cereals that are nutritious to mix in water or milk for a perfect breakfast; instant noodles or rice that aid people going to rural areas for rescue where limited food resources are available; books written by Master Cheng Yen or by other brothers and sisters, etc. All sort of publications help to propagate good deeds so we know that there are good people out there helping others.

The main branch of the Tzu Chi Buddhist Foundation is based in Hwa-Lien, a city located at the south-eastern part of Taiwan Island. It is a rural area where there is little industrial or business activity. Masters residing at Hwa-Lien, the main branch, do not rely on others to support their daily living.

The funds raised by members or by other sources are allocated to the four missions and/or eight footprints. This is to ensure that all the funds raised have gone directly to the ones in need. My mother has entrusted the charity works; hence she has donated thousands of dollars over the years, because she knows the funds have been properly managed and distributed. Donating money to others was one thing she would never have been able to do before, because she was so tight with money. "This money has gone to the ones who are really in need," she says—and she is proud of it.

For years she has still lived a very frugal life, and she saves every single cent to either donate to others or to utilize for running the family. My mother has had her heart opened to the world and she loves getting involved with the charity.

One thing for which I'm very grateful to my mother is the fact that she never raised any negative comments about my friends and/ or mates—not even about those friendships which did not sound promising. She always welcomes my friends home and talks to them. Later on I realized that there were people my mother did not really appreciate much, but she never ever badmouthed them in front of me.

She just wanted to her daughter to be back within her arms. This is the wisdom she adopted from Buddha's wisdom: to treat everyone with mercy, to be understanding, and to be generous about love. She never puts me in a position of comparison with others. To her, the most important thing is to have her daughter happy and healthy.

This long process of learning has given my mother and me another pathway to reunite. We've both grown under Buddha's wisdom. We went from doing things on our different pathways to holding our hands together and sharing. Thank you, Master Cheng Yen, and Buddha!

CHAPTER 10

Sometimes Things Aren't That Bad . . . .

Imagination is everything.
It is the preview of life's coming attractions.
~Albert Einstein

When everything went so wrong, I started imagining miracles happening. I pictured beautiful things surrounding me. Magically, beautiful things started coming into my life . . . . All it takes is a bit of imagination and trust—the trust that you will be OK.

I will always remember my high school teacher told me one quote: *Smile, and the world smiles with you. Cry, cry alone.*

I still consider myself lucky to have had my darkest hours living in Sydney, because Sydney has the most beautiful blue sky that could make life a little bit easier during those bad patches. I started learning fake-smiling, hoping that would work to ease my pain after all the drama in my life. I needed to learn to laugh. Yes, you heard me right, I needed to learn HOW TO LAUGH or SMILE. Or maybe I was simply sick of being sick, sick of being sad?

After not having too much luck in finding friends within my peer group, and also not having too much association with my family, I developed a very unique hobby . . . talking to strangers on the street, or, even more, cheering babies on the street! I could easily hook up with people on the street and talk to strangers. It was my hobby. It became my habit. Well, when you go home and have no one to talk to either at home or at school, you still need to mingle with people, you still need to talk, you still need to associate with others. So the way I achieved that I was to talk to people randomly on the street. Trust me, it is a fun process. Talking to strangers on the street alleviates daily pressure. Over the years, I have been able to cheer people up on the train. It was a traveller's hobby and it was fun. I became quite good at giving insightful talks to people when I was doing some volunteering work.

It started one day when I saw a mother with her little baby in a pram. I started giggling at the baby and made her laugh. The mother was a very friendly person and she started telling me about her story and how she managed to come to Sydney from Europe; being a full-time mother when she had to look after a baby was not easy. I started cheering her baby up when the baby was crying. I played hide and seek, made silly faces, or played with her little toys. I tried every single way I could think of to cheer up the baby. By the time they got off the train, the baby was anxiously looking for me, backwards and forwards. It wasn't until then that I realized I had the talent to cheer babies up. Now I have managed to extend the age range from young toddlers to teenage girls as well.

Believe me, the baby's smile is one of the most beautiful things on earth. Their angelic smiles will take pressures away in no time! They are so pure and innocent.

This habit has given me great joy when taking public transport, especially on the train or MRT (in Taiwan they call it the MRT, or MTR in Japan or Singapore). I could easily talk to people on the train without offending people or scaring them away. All it takes is a friendly and sincere smile.

I remember that when I was in Taiwan, there was this handicapped five-year-old boy with his grandmother. The granny was obviously upset with the boy's condition and had a frown on her face. The handicapped boy was having a tantrum; he was crying hard on the MRT and it became quite disturbing to the other passengers. It was obvious that the granny felt quite ashamed about it. She kept scolding the boy, telling him not to do this and that.

Well, a little boy like that would not be equipped to control his temper, unless you did something about it, so I approached him with a huge smile. I made sure he felt safe and happy talking to me. I also started cheering him up by playing fingers with him. I think I might have used every single resource I had at the time to cheer him up— my fingers, something in my purse that has smiley faces, and most importantly, my facial expressions and my warm gestures.

Usually the toddler's sixth sense is very strong. Toddlers know who is positive and approachable, and vice versa. When you gain their trust, they will start reciprocate positively. This mindset really worked. The boy stopped his tantrum and started laughing with me. It was a great feeling to know that I could make people happy, even strangers on the train.

This sort of hobby extended to different areas in my life. I became good at mingling with my friends' babies. I became quite good at coaching people's kids. One day I had the chance to look after my friends' kids, ages ten and thirteen. The two boys had different problems. The older boy had problems focusing, but he was a smart boy. The mother was a single mother who had always used scolding as her way of teaching her kids. The mother might have exerted her own pressure on her kids unconsciously, which is understandable.

So when I was supervising the children, I never scolded them. Instead, I encouraged them to say whatever they wanted to say.

The older boy could never finish his homework. He was simply mucking around with things that he did not want to do. He was avoiding doing his homework since he was not getting positive feedback from doing it. So when he did not want to do his homework and was avoiding it, I simply sat down and rationalized with him. I asked him, "Do you know what will happen if you have not finished your homework when your mother returns?"

He nodded his head; he knew he would get into trouble if he did not complete his homework by the time his mother returned. So I followed my statement by saying, "So would you like to see your mother's unhappy face and have her start to scold you?" He swayed his head. Knowing the repercussions of not having the homework done, he was able to finish his homework on time. I never scolded him with any condescending tone. I was talking to him on his own level. At the same time, I was trying to tell him if he did not finish his homework on time, no one would be happy—the mother; the boy who would be scolded by his mother; and me, who would be accused not doing my job properly.

As soon as he started sitting at his desk to work on his homework, the second challenge came along. He was scribbling on his notebook instead of doing his homework. I knew he was trying to get my attention, so I did not let it get on my nerves. If I got angry, then I lost the game. I asked him patiently, "Do you think it looks nice with your CRAZY scribbling?" He began giggling. He was being so cheeky, and felt a bit ashamed to answer my question. So I looked at him with a stern look. "So tell me if you really think this looks NICE." He knew I was serious and was not up for jokes anymore. Then I turned my stern face on and told him to do his homework properly.

I did not get to see if he had done his homework properly. I knew that day that the primary task for him was to have his homework done on time. I needed him to not procrastinate. It was a good achievement. We can probably deal with his quality of work later on if there are subsequent sessions with him, but the primary thing is to get his mindset right.

That afternoon we made a great achievement, having his homework completed on time. I did not care if it was done properly at that point; I was taking it one step at a time. So the little boy ended up finishing his homework earlier than we thought, and he got to play with his favourite game when there was extra time left. We were all winners. Everyone was happy.

Perhaps there is a bonus to my having rebelled; I was able to perceive things from the rebel's angle. I was able to penetrate angles from the kids without giving condescending comments. I was able to communicate! When the communication door is open, then the chances of success are greater. I cannot emphasize the importance of communication. You will always need to have the doors open, and things can be done more promptly and smoothly that way.

I remember that during the very sad days of my life back in years eleven and twelve, my teacher told me one western quote: "Laugh the world laughs with you, but cry and you cry alone." At that point in time I was living alone. It was the loneliest time of my life. I had no friends at school and every day I came home to face the cold bricks without having anyone to talk to. That quote really served a purpose at the right time. It was such a great quote to me that it has lived with me all these years. It wasn't until then that I started "learning" to smile or/ and laugh, even if I was feeling so depressed and unwell.

Remembering the sad days of your life is not a pleasant sensation. It was one of those days when you did not know how to answer people when they asked you, "How are you?" You see, when you are not feeling well from the inside and that has extended to your physical health, I can assure you that means, "I am NOT good." At the point of feeling unworthy, unwilling to live, hopeless, resentful, etc., all that negative energy would be more than sufficient to strangle you.

I knew I needed help. I was not smiling or talking. It was unhealthy. So when you are desperate for help, you start seeking and researching. Luckily I forced myself to start laughing, smiling, or doing something silly to ensure I was happier, or at least I pretended to be. It was a very hard lesson, to learn how to smile and be happy again. The learning curve sounds ridiculous, but yes, I did start learning to be happy again.

I started picking up trivial things that could possibly make me happy. Cheering babies up on the train was one of them. I started looking at the sky with its different curves and shapes, imagining what they resembled. I daydreamed of happy things that could possibly come to me to cheer me up. Although they did not really help my issues, they did add a bit of spark in my life. This habit also helped me while I was going through the dark hours of my life. It gave me faith that there will always be light at the end of the tunnel.

As mentioned earlier, my father suffers from unstable mood swing. In simple terms it means that someone has an unstable mental state,. The mental state varies from euphoric to depressed stages, yet the person is unable to control it. When my father is very depressed, he can sometimes not talk for a period of time, and will stare at some certain things for a long time without having any interaction with this world. He is in the state of mind in which he is NOT there, nor here. I needed to provoke him at some certain level, to wake him up! To achieve that, I need to act silly, to play games with him, to poke him, to tease him with words, or even to tickle him—whatever I could do to cheer him up. He could be sitting there for hours not moving, so I would always act silly and talk silly to him.

This later on became the very way in which we communicate. For instance, when I take him to the place he goes by taxi, before he takes off, I would have to remind him, "Please do not talk to strangers," or, "Please do not scare the strangers away!"—all sorts of funny and silly senseless jokes to grab his attention. As a result of that, my father and I have become best buddies. It was great fun at home.

The pair of us would do things behind my mother's back. Due to my mother's extreme thrifty behaviour, she would not go with us on outings which she felt were luxurious. Well, a simple meal may seem quite luxurious to my mother. My father and I would hang out eating things that were simply not allowed at home. It was quite an adventure. We both had an agreement not to tell my mother where we had been, and we were not to come home and get ourselves into trouble by telling my mother how much we had spent! You see, in my family, spending money is equivalent to committing a crime! So to go out having a great dinner had to be done secretly. My mother, in this case, is quite good.

She never really asked what my father and I did or ate in our secret outing dates. It became a secret between my father and me.

We would go shopping and then it was very conventional for him to scrutinize the items we were looking for. He would pick on the shopkeepers and tell them how these items were really in bad quality and they were simply too expensive. It was his personality to criticise things, but I could easily turn the tension into humour there by poking at his nose or snitching his faces. The shopkeepers would be easily distracted and amused by this scene. It was quite fun. People love to hang around with bubbly happy people like me.

Recently my father told me that he is learning how to sing. I can assure you that we do not have singing genes in our family; neither of my parents could sing properly. Nonetheless I was quite happy to learn my father was picking up some sort of hobby, such as singing. It would be quite fun to see my father harassing others with his squeaky voice.

Whenever I called my father, I needed to bring some sort of joyful voices to him. It became my hobby to tease him. "So how did you go killing animals, or what sort of animals have you been slaughtering?" (In Chinese language, if you have a terrible voice or play really bad instruments, killing animals can be metaphorically describing how badly it sounds.) That is how I tease my father. That is my way of showing my endearment to him. I like him to be happy. I love his smile. I miss his joyful smile. It brings me great joy to see my father's smile and happy face.

I love bringing people joy, as is said by the quote, "Laugh, and the world will laugh with you." Unfortunately, I still sometimes cry alone. However those cheerful moments have actually guided me to be optimistic when I really need them to enlighten those shadowy parts of my life.

When you start imagining things coming to fruition, you start seeking new ways. Communication is the same thing. You will need to start from somewhere, somewhere in your mind. Be patient with yourself and the surroundings.

CHAPTER 11

"*I Am Willing to Change for My Daughter,*" *Says My Tiger Mom*

A peace is of the nature of a conquest;
for then both parties nobly are subdued,
and neither party loser.
~William Shakespeare

Over the years, my mother and I have learned to establish a harmonious relationship. We team up to deal with issues and matters. She is no longer controlling. She has learned to listen to me in depth and also to be included in my life. She started seeing things from my perspective instead of monopolizing everything. I guess we have both grown on personal levels, and the communication seems a lot easier when both of us are on the same page.

Since my mother does not do much shopping, the charity became our common ground to do things together. We have lots of insights to share when we are both involved in our charity. The charity has established a bridge facilitating our understandings of each other. All of the sudden there is lots to share with each other.

As mentioned before, my mother is a very thrifty person. Just about everything she talks about is money and money and money. Well, she came from a very poor background, and her background made her this way. I understand where she is coming from, but her extremely thrifty behavior used to drive me up to the wall (and it still does to this date). She is a great mother. There is no doubt that the family's financial stability arose from her extreme thrifty behaviour. However there is always a certain extent of resentfulness that lies inside my heart.

As a young girl, I was never able to shop with her, and could not discuss all the girly private conversations. She is the Asian version of "Scrooge," who would never spend any extra penny for anything, i.e.: cosmetics, clothing, and all the accessories that girls and females would spend money on. We used to joke with each other that, if all the customers were like my mother, then all the cosmetic companies and the fashion design industry would collapse!

On the other hand, my mother is very wise about her investments. She saved every single penny to acquire property investments, which she recognizes as being a step of establishing wealth.

The most incredible thing about her is that she was able to afford expensive private school fees just to ensure I was well educated. She regarded education as the primary key to send me here to Australia.

My mother also financed an English tutor for me. This tutor of mine was a vice president in a public high school. Due to his high social status, he not only charged a little bit more than the other tutors, ie: he was charging us $45 per hour instead of the average price of $30 to$35 dollars per hour, but he also had his own very unique way of showing me how English literature works. He would not take any ordinary students, but would only take someone who had the potential to improve. I was lucky to be his student. He showed me how to see things from a very different angle and how to read English on a daily basis. He actually taught me to immerse the language as part of my life. I have learned a very unique perspective from him in the process of learning English.

My mother's very way to ensure I received a proper education has really made me who I am. For this, I owe her great appreciation.

Twenty years ago, most of the immigrants coming to Australia were quite wealthy. Most of them had acquired a certain amount of wealth in order to be able to come to Australia. However, my family was not one of them. In order for my mother to support the family, she purchased a house and sub-rented to others. She did this to keep the finances going in Australia so that she did not have to bring money from Taiwan. Sub-renting also meant that my mother could find someone to look after me.

During those years I went through tremendous mental trauma that no one was able to picture. Even up to this day I still feel dismay from those years of growing up as a teenager. To live with all sorts of different strangers, and to see them coming and going exerted a huge amount of uncertainty on my mental state. There were lots of disputes from the tenants and my mother, simply we had different living background.

My mother used to curse at me when things went wrong. What things? Everything. When the house needed repairs, the stove was too old, the swimming pool equipment need replacement—for all of this she scolded me. When the tenants moved out, she pointed fingers at me for being so uneasy to get along with. When the swimming pool needed filtering replacements she scolded me badly. She was basically exerting her enormous uncertainly and insecurity about money on me.

I was only a teenager, and I was in a foreign country. At that point my relationship with my mother went frozen. Sadly enough, she doesn't remember any of those incidents now, but those incidents are etched in my mind. It is almost like a nail carved in your heart, and it hurts. It hurts every time you think about it. It hurts when I visit the old house once in a while.

Unfortunately my mother never admits to anything she did. I presume she does not want to know about it, nor can she even think about it? I don't know. I am not sure. After a certain number of years, she did subtly mention that she actually put her head in the sand so she does not like to think about it. She never thought that what has been done was wrong. Or perhaps that was the best way she could think of at that point of time? I presume that she did her very best to support me in those years. Perhaps that was NOT the best way, but that was the BEST she could do.

My best friend even pointed out that my mother had done what other mothers cannot do. She sacrificed herself and left her little baby in another country so that her little baby was able to receive a better education. She was trying to provide me an alternative avenue so that I was able to can get western education, so that I could have more opportunities in the future. Learning to speak proper English in Asia was a biggie to the Asian community (and it still is to this day); it means you will have better chances of having a secure job in the future.

As a young adult now I can understand where she was coming from. She must have suffered a lot, too, to leave her little baby overseas and bear the thought of not seeing me. I never confirmed this thought with her. Every time I started this topic, she stayed silent and reserved with her feelings, saying that the primary imperative thing at the time was to secure the family finances.

I still remember whenever she came to Sydney to visit, she always filled the fridge before she left, just to make sure that I was well fed for another few months. She was always making all of these Asian dumplings and buns. She worked hard. I remember that she used to make the dumplings with her tears at the kitchen. She was wiping tears whilst cooking. For a long time I could not have dumplings or buns simply because I associated those foods with sorrow.

Many times she did not teach me how to work things out, but instead carried on doing things for me. The lack of guidance, teaching, and communication had resulted in tension between my mother and myself. As I had been quite secluded in my teenage years, I found it difficult to associate with people in a mutual way. I looked at things in an extreme manner and saw them as being either yes or no; grey area to me could sometimes be quite disturbing.

To sidetrack a bit, later on when I joined the workforce with female superiors, I often associate them as mother figures. Amazingly I often found my bosses who shared similar attributes with my mother. The hate and love relationship between my bosses and myself could be quite similar in so many ways as the relationship between me and my mother. It is interesting.

Yes, deep inside, I know she tries her very best to be a good mother. Now, when I think back, I still consider myself lucky to have survived all these years. And yes, she did her very BEST to ensure the family finances were secure. But what she did not do was to explain to me what was going on, or that she herself was bewildered at that point of time. That was my only resentment towards her.

Of course I went mad. Of course I rebelled. I was unable to express my frustration, so my refusal to talk to her became endless. She was also reluctant to talk to me. She regarded me as a teenage rebellious girl who would go on and spend excessive amounts of money without consideration.

Balloon flying off into the sky

I was walking down on the road the other day, and I saw this balloon flying off into the blue sky with the string attached. Somehow it was dispatched into the sky and lost its connection to the land. It got me thinking: If a person is metaphorically like a balloon and does not have a string attached, would it just fly off into the sky? Isn't it like people who have lost their connections to their origin and wander off? They lose stability. And yes, there may be lots of freedom attained, but it is directionless.

All human beings need this sense of stability as the core feeling, and this core is FAMILY. As for the old cliché, FAMILY stands for "Father And Mother, I Love You." The spontaneity may be attractive, but directionless freedom can be detrimental. People without direction in life are driving to nowhere, and the proper word for this is "LOST."

I was once in that spectrum. That sense of being nowhere hits me hard. The loss of focus and the sense of insecurity chill me from the inside; it is cold. Sometimes I still get emotional about things that I have missed, and this sense of hollowness fills me.

The difference between lucky and being blessed

Later on I realized that there is a difference between being lucky and being blessed. Being lucky is simply that sometimes things just turn out to be lucky once in a lifetime. Sometimes you are just lucky that there is no waiting queue in front of you. That happens spontaneously.

But being blessed is when you develop the ability to appreciate things around you; that is when you are sincerely blessed. It happens when you know how to look at the bright side even when things are turning back on you. You learn to look at things from the reverse cycle, like J.F. Kennedy used to say: "When written in Chinese, the word "crisis" is composed of two characters. One represents danger and the other represents opportunity."

I began to perceive opportunities in my life when things might look superficially quite bad, but I call them life calling cards. I was able to eradicate issues underneath, hence finding the perfect way out. That is when I started thinking: It happened to me many times in my life, but it can turn out to be an amazing turning point in my life. I appreciate these opportunities with love.

I developed a very minor heart symptom called MVP—Mitrial Valve Prolapse. It is a valvular heart disease characterized by the displacement of an abnormally thickened mitral valve leaflet into the left atrium during systole. In simple terms, the heart is not pumping properly as the valve is lacking energy. It is usually caused by tension or some sort of mental distress.

The onset started after my best friend Noriko went off overseas, attempting suicide. She tried to kill herself but did not end up dying. However, because of some personal issues, she refused to talk to me for at least fifteen months. It is hard to explain. When someone is not well, the questions, "How are you," or "Are you okay?" may even trigger sorrow for them. Noriko could not confront the question. She was not well, and she was unable to express her feelings. She could not tell people that she was unwell. She needed time alone.

My heart was broken as a result of her leaving. Not being able to talk to her or to know how she was doing really made me sad. My heart condition MVP had terrible onset so that it felt like there was no tomorrow or even the next second! Unfortunately it was still considered mild and there is no medication for it. My heart condition was only symptomatic. However, I remember suffering for one month feeling unwell. The fact that I could not breathe properly was really devastating. The struggle to breathe was terrifying. It was not a good sensation at all. I almost felt like I was dying at some point. This symptomatic situation lasted more than one month before it was stabilized.

I went to a Chinese herbalist for help. She is a great Chinese herbal doctor and she treated it well. However the heart condition seemed to always come back. The reoccurrence of the symptoms made both the herbal doctor and me realize that there was a reason behind this illness. She told me, "Julia, you have a very deep sorrow. If you don't find a way to sort this out, my treatments to you will only be temporary."

Because my best friend Noriko refused to talk to me for some reason, I no longer had her contact details anymore. I had to reconnect with her other friend to pass on words for me. I said to him, "If you happen to talk to Noriko, can you please let her know that I really don't know if I can live to the next day—my heart condition is killing me. Can you please let her know that I am thinking of her?"

Within the next few weeks she was back in contact with me. Within the next ten weeks I flew up to Japan to see her. Amazingly, over the few days of visiting her, my heart condition did not come back and bite me. My heart behaved. I am now reassured that the sorrow or had caused my physical stress.

This MVP has given me the chance to reconnect back to Noriko, my dearest friend. I appreciate how it taught me, in a very different way, to perceive life. "When there is a danger, there is an opportunity," said J. F. Kennedy. I was reconnected with my best friend.

Believe in yourself that you will be okay, and you will be perfectly okay.

Believe in yourself that you are EXCELLENT, and you are EXCELLENT.

There is always a way out, should there be challenges in life.

CHAPTER 12

Sometimes All You Need Is an Apology, I Am Sorry

With a mini series you can give
the story a proper sense of pacing,
a proper sense of closure.
~Garth Ennis

After all the incidents that happened in Sydney, and despite knowing my mother had done her very best to keep things intact, I still demand an answer. I needed an apology. I needed to acknowledge my pain. I needed to tell my mother I was hurt.

At some point I realized that my mother will always be her, and I remain the one victimized and trapped in the years I had been left alone in Sydney. I went through all the rationales of how and why she managed things in her way, but I was still trapped. I knew she had done her best, and leaving me in Sydney in a huge house with all different strangers (tenants) was possibly the best modality she could come up with at the time. However, knowing is one thing. To forgive is another matter.

A long battle after staying with my mother and being assured that she is a loving mother was not enough. I still needed something else. It was like a closure. I was THAT stubborn. Every time my mother and I had a discussion about all the arrangements she had managed, things would go really badly. It usually turned out to be a bad argument, and I felt terrible after that. Usually I would have a tearful face with my heart broken, because they were terrible memories to me. That was part of the terrible times in my life. The reassurance from my mother did not seem sufficient, because all of the devastation I had lived through was true and real. Any discussion about it would trigger the pain. As sad as it is, the sad memories just live within me.

It was part of me. I am sorry, there is nothing anyone could do to wipe them out. It will always be part of me. *So what can I do about it?* I asked myself. I went through all the conventional advice that people would tell you, like forgive and forget, let go—you name it, I have done them all. Well, at least I think I have. I've tried all of the conventional mental mindsets that can transform your negativity. I went through that process. Unfortunately, regardless how many times I tried to practice that in me, it would not work. I wonder why . . . .

One day I pushed that button again with my mother. As part of the convention, she did not solicit herself as the faulty one. That attitude infuriated me. I simply needed an answer. I threw things at her, shouted at her. I just need her to acknowledge that she had done something wrong. Eventually I sort of gave in. I begged her to apologize. I said to her, "Can you simply apologize? It will make me feel a lot better. You may not know why and how you are apologizing, simply because you don't think it was wrong to leave me alone back in Australia, but I really need your apology to make it up for myself."

For my sake, my mother apologized, not even knowing what she was apologizing for. But she did it because she knew it would make me feel better. After the traumatic event, I could not go to work the next day. I had to call in a sick leave. She actually rang me up to see how I was recuperating. I could sense that she knew I was suffering, without knowing exactly how.

Amazingly, after her apology I felt better. Somehow the grudges in my mind seemed to fade away a little. The wound started scarring off. The wound started healing in opposed to the previously weeping.

It is quite amazing what my mother did. She has risen above her conventional viewpoint. Like one of my best friends, Charlene, says, "You want right or peace, choose one." My mother chose peace, and it worked. Love is all about compromise.

My wound started healing better. My mother's apology was like a note of acknowledgment. Knowing that my pain means a great deal to me, this gave me a great sense of being understood. This is part of the closure process.

My mother has always been very schematic about her financial status. She is really good at planning her monetary status, but not me. She never really taught me how to manage money, or should I say she has always been able to manage the family finances, so I just leave everything to her? On the other hand, she has always been controlling and so thrifty with things that I simply do not agree with her totally. However, I still cannot deny the fact that she is really good with money. I am nowhere close to her way of strategically managing money, or the way she saves money. It is simply not me.

I still went on my rebellious ways to spend money. I simply cannot do whatever my mother asked me to. I am sorry. I am sorry, Mom, I cannot be the Miss Goodie Goodie you expect me to be. I need to simply make myself align with who I am. You will see one day that I will be successful and fine. Everything will turn out to be perfectly fine, maybe not exactly the way you want me to be, but I will always be your daughter, the one who loves you.

After regaining the assurance of love from my mother, trust and belief have served as the foundation of strength within me. I have faith in myself—I will be fine.

CHAPTER 13
Redefine Love

Only divine love bestows the keys of knowledge.
~Arthur Rimbaud

Love is a very interesting word. It is a verb, it is an act—a divine one. This is possibly the lesson all humankind should learn, and will, throughout their lifetime journeys in any forms.

It took my mother and me a long time to redefine "LOVE". How long? Approximately ten to fifteen years, progressively. The Chinese character of love愛 has a symbol of heart in the middle, and beneath it is a hand. It is situated in the middle to ensure it is in the proper position; never let it down or allows your heart to fall. It means to carry someone in their heart with caution.

My mother started to realize that nagging would not serve the purpose anymore after joining the Tzu Chi Buhhist Foundation. Master Cheng Yen taught us the real meaning of love. Through Master's words of wisdom, my mother learned to execute love in a proper manner. She started to appreciate things in life with a positive attitude. She started to learn to respect, to understand, and to let go of fear and resentment.

She started realizing that I am no longer her property or someone who she can dominate upon. I am actually an independent individual but I am someone who originated from her womb. Even though she has given birth to me, that does not necessarily mean that she owns me. It was a huge step for her. As a domineering person like herself, she has done very well to learn and accept such lessons.

At the time when she was looking after the family she had to become a very tough person. Her strength and matriarchal character allowed her to look after the family, including its financial status, in one piece. Inevitably she had done very well when the family was going through hurdles. When she had no one to rely on but herself, she took every single step in scrutiny to ensure the family stayed together and the bills were paid on time.

I am a strong believer in the book, "The Secret," by Ronda Byrne. My mother has a vision of what has been described in "The Secret;" she had achieved everything she wanted in her life. She had achieved financial security with her extreme thrifty behaviour. She managed to support the family without having to ask someone else for support, even when my father suffered from his unstable mood swing. Her strong mindset has established what she wanted in life, and that has come into fruition perfectly. Financial security has always been the primary key for her.

However, she still got lost. I remember one day seeing her weeping. She said to me, "When I was young, I had nothing. I so wished to have a roof over my head, bills paid, and secure finances. Now I have everything—a husband, two kids, a few properties, and my finances are okay—but why am I NOT happy?"

That scene struck me. It made me think and reflect. How bad can it be when you have achieved everything you wanted in life and then you still feel lost and resented? How can that happen? And why? Yes, why?

Well, when you work very hard and focus on what you wanted, sometimes you lose sight. My mother used every single cell of hers to save money, as much as she could. Somewhere along the way she had gone beyond limits. She also got very scornful about others spending excessively. She was very judgmental about when and why to spend money, even judging some other strangers.

At some point I think that in her mind, spending even a little more money was viewed as being a crime in the family. Anything that related to money was NOT allowed. Unfortunately a lot of things are related to money. In her mind, everything is measured by money. There is no additional value to life, but money.

It is understandable that she had to count every single cent she spent and be very careful with it. But the fact that she got judgemental, that got side—tracked. What I mean by side-tracked is that she does not spend money on leisure or even on some necessary medical expenses such as dentals. Anything which will require money to be spent will not go forward at all. So, no going out dining, no personal leisure, no manicures or pedicures, no expensive cosmetics, and no shopping (of course). Frugal is her middle name. She does not even purchase any drinks off the street, but goes home and drinks water! When we were younger and lived under her supervision, life could be tough and we did not have much freedom. There were materialistic things that kids yearn for, but these were not attainable most of the time when we were kids.

At some point she would even use malicious words to describe people spending excessively. It was out of her sense of inferiority. Deep down inside, she is still the one without too much money to spend—after years of striving to get out of poverty and having made a tremendous achievement, she still has a mindset in that she is fearful of living in poverty. It is arbitrary that she lives under means.

So let's be fair, but this great contrast makes little sense. On one hand, she did whatever she could do to ensure the family's financial status was secure, but on the other hand, no one in the family is allowed to have a bit of pleasure if we are to head out for a bit of leisure, meaning that spending a little bit of money can be criminal. Eventually my brother and myself drifted away from her because we know her ideas on money. It was kind of sad. From memory, my mother hardly had any chance to ever go out dining with the family members. We did not really share too much of shopping fun as the other mother and daughters did. If we ever did go out to dine, it would be quite tense; again the food ordered would be heavily judged on how much it cost.

Over the years, my mother changed a lot. After my brother and I had grown and started working, the financial burden had gone down a lot. She no longer needed to stress over the source of income. My father has not been working since he was fifty-five-years old. The mood swings and his inability to keep up with the world have been tough on him. Sadly my father's health condition required him to be hospitalized to ensure his mental state was stable. He has been hospitalized for approximately three to five times over the period of the last ten years.

Since the stress level of finances had gone down a fair bit, my mother has diverted her attention to the charity work at the Tzu Chi Buddhist Foundation. She has acquired a great sense of achievement from her participation. She learned the wisdom of Buddha's words and how to communicate with people better. She found meaning in life through charity, by helping people, and by attending community works.

In the process of her charity participation, she started redefining her life. The change was sensational. She realized how important it is for her to change. When you lose sight of what you want, then that is time to start redefining your life and making certain changes. The changes starts from changing your mindset. My mother started that process when she joined the Tzu Chi Buddhist Foundation. Through Buddha's wise words and Master Cheng Yen's teaching, my mother learned to give instead of keeping everything she has gotten. She learned to be selfless and put words of wisdom into action. She shares her heart, her emotions, and even her wealth with the community.

She now understands that giving does not mean losing but gaining. The more you give, the more rewarding it is if you are doing in the right way. According to Buddha's wisdom, it is imperative to expect nothing when giving, because you give and share out of your personal will. If you expect something in return, then the whole essence of giving is lost. This is how my mother learned most of her Buddhism practice. She learned to be selfless. It was hard but she bit the bullet and took every single step to learn. Remember, my mother is a very strong-willed person.

Once my mother took the first step in getting out of the door, she started embracing the crowd and the people in the community. It all started with one thought: she wanted her daughter back. Unimaginably, it expanded to a whole different spectrum. She got to see the world from a very different angle. She was no longer tunnel-visioned about things, things only tied to money. There are so many things to know and to learn, and different angles to look at things apart from her old money lenses. She opened her heart. Happiness has become her middle name.

A lot of times we learn things whilst we cruise along life. Being devoted to charity work is the same thing. It was not until years later that my mother realized that the person who benefited the most from the whole process was herself. She learned the wisdom of giving, and the reward is countless. Instead of scrutinizing how much money is spent, she started to realize that there are other things to cherish. Then she started to redefine love.

In Buddhism, the primary essence of philosophy is cause and effect. What you plant as seeds will result in what you get in fruition, regardless of good or bad. My mother had gone to root out what needed to be rectified, and then the redefinition process would start.

Love is about respect, selflessness, and giving. It is not about how much you spend on things, but how much effort you put in. Money can be put into numbers, but not love. Love is countless. Love is endless. Love can expand beyond what you can expect, because it has no boundaries.

My mother started respecting who I am as an individual. She realized that I am no longer the same person I was when I left Taiwan at the age of fourteen. The unique circumstances made me a very different person. I have a very different mindset than the rest of the others. The angles from which I see things are very different and unique. She took me in a very different way after I went back to Taiwan to reside. One more important factor—she does not want to lose me again.

One day when my best friend Noriko visited, my mother told her, "Julia is no longer the one I sent her overseas to study. She is now a very different person. Regardless, I love her. I accept the way she is NOW." Whenever I had problems with my mother and discussed the issues with Noriko(my best friend), she would always remind me that my mother had changed herself to reaccept just who I was. This is something a lot of Asian parents cannot do, but my mother did. For that, my mother is truly amazing. She no longer enforces her ideas on me anymore. She tries not to impose her opinions on me. She just accepted the way that I am, and how I am. There were a lot of things she started looking at from a very different angle.

I was in Taiwan for twelve years. I was bombarded with a huge amount of cultural shock when I first got back. The Asian way of collection and the westernized way of individualism really got me convoluted. Being back in Taiwan, I had gone through not only cultural shock but also role changes. I was a student being so naïve about the working environment, and joining the workforce back in Taiwan with a totally different mindset had indeed stunned me.

Bear in mind that I spent most of my teenage years, the years which form your mindset, in Sydney. The mindset in Taiwan is totally different from how I was educated in Sydney. There was a lot of ambivalence and confusion. I returned to Taiwan not based on my personal will. I had to go back simply because I was very sick. My mental state was unwell. I was no longer able to deal with things on my own, including the drama of the house, car, education, and the work force. I needed to be with my family. Being along to combat with mundane life was no longer accessible to me.

So the first five years back in Taiwan were a huge torment to me. I could not get along with people at work. I did not have a sense of direction because I did not know what my life was heading to. I had no real life skills but a bit of English, better spoken than the local people. That was it. It was a jungle out there, a rough one when I first got back. It was like walking in the mist; the sense of directionless and lack of security in future was hard. I have always regarded English as being only a medium, a bridge to communicate, but not a life skill. There is always something additional to learn apart from being able to speak or write English well. I needed more. However, in Taiwan, being able to speak or write proper English is considered a skill.

My mother played a very helpful role when I was in Taiwan. She reminded me of where I came from, where my roots are. She also showed me the cultural way to communicate locally in Taiwan, something that I had missed and forgotten over the years of growing up in Sydney. When I needed help, she was there sitting with me going through things that had gone so wrong at work. She provided great guidance patiently and showed me how things worked in Taiwan culturally. She was there to share things with me. She became a good listener instead of a dictator. When I was having trouble at work, she was there to hug me and made sure that I was getting a good night's sleep following a stressful day at work. Her support meant a lot to me.

It makes a huge difference when someone is no longer judgemental on things, especially when she is your mother. Her perspective was objective and insightful. There were things she could pick up from my conversation with her. By talking it out, she was able to see things from my angle instead of judging me with a biased viewpoint.

My relationship with my mother had risen to the collaborative level. We worked together through problems or hurdles. We helped each other out. You know what? The tension gradually dissolved. Things are heading in the right direction. We are both happier as days go by.

Respect is such an important factor in keeping the relationship in harmony. She respects who I am, and I respect who she is. There is less reinforcement of things that she wants me to do or become. She allows me to be who I am, and how I want to be. It is interesting, isn't it? That sometimes a kid yearns for the mother's consent and approval of what and who she wants to be? If I need permission from my mother to be who I want to be, then I am quite liberal in that sense, well, as long as I keep my finances under control and be safe.

In Asia, people greet each other by asking you either if you have eaten or what your marital status is. This is a part of the start-up conversation, even with strangers or relatives you have not met in a while. It is considered to be a sign of endearment or caring when these questions are raised. To me, these sorts of personal and critical questions seem to be rude and blunt. To my resentment, these personal questions have always been raised to me in Taiwan. I really didn't like it. It was quite personal. And it can be quite confronting or complicated to be asked those questions. On the contrary, my mother never asked me these personal questions. She just made sure I got home everyday in one piece, nice and happy. The only thing that she cares about is my financial status, whether I am capable of being financially independent, and if I can support myself. She is being practical and realistic.

I appreciate how my mother took the effort to change. It is through her that I've seen for myself that, with her support, I can grow as a person.

CHAPTER 14

Unconditional Love and Never–Ending Hugs

Love is the great miracle cure.
Loving ourselves works miracles in our lives.
~Louise L. Hay

I lived in Sydney, Australia for eight years without much of my parents' presence. The absence of my parents' love for eight years had created a huge hole in my heart, along with a sense of insecurity and loss. I have been feeling fearful of losing them again. I was very afraid.

After I went back to Taiwan to reside, I had tried everything to fill that hole. There were times I went to my parents' bedside, sometimes just to check their pulses to see if they were still breathing (it is silly, I know). I loved waking either my father or my mother up by their bedside. It was a way to assure myself that they were still alive, and I still had them with me. My inner child refused to grow up. There was the need to compensate for things I had yearned for whilst growing up. The things I missed during my teenage years.

When you need something so much, you search for it, and you ask for it, and you hold on to it. I never got used to the lifestyle in Taiwan. I never got used to the social norms. I could never fit into it. However

I was living in Taipei for twelve years straight, simply because I was unable to get out of the comfort zone and my parents' nurture. It was something I still want to get back from my teenage years.

When you are not ready for the move or grow up, you will find a million excuses not to get out. Initially I mistakenly thought that the reasons I could not leave were due to financial reasons. Later on I realized it was something else: I simply refused to grow up. I needed to stay with my parents as much as I could. When there were times that I simply could not adjust the lifestyle in Taiwan, I could comfort myself that at least I had my parents with me. Yes, and I secretly went to their bedsides to reconfirm their pulses, checking that they were still alive.

The twelve years of staying with my parents really served a purpose. We managed to celebrate Father's Day, Mother's Day, and my birthday together every year with cakes and singing. Finally there were things we did as a family to celebrate together. Sometimes it could be quite challenging when my mother's thrifty habits would interfere with any sort of leisure. However, I tried to hide things from her—for example, the price of anything needed to be eliminated. It is just not the right way to communicate in my family. The price tag has to be cut, otherwise it becomes problematic. In my mother's eyes, anything excessive is considered expensive or unnecessary.

My mother rephrased the word "love" to me in the twelve years of my stay in Taiwan. She kept the door open for me all those years and made sure our communication bridge was open. When I was facing traumatic things at work, she would always reinforce her support at night with a warm hug. She told me not to worry about not keeping the job, but being collected was the main key. She was there to assure me that I had remained calm and things would turn out OK. When I look back on those dramatic years of having chaotic issues with my boss and colleagues, I can still remember the temperature of her hug and the scent coming from her warm body.

I remember one day I was dismissed from my job in Taiwan. The boss's son had come back to Taiwan to take over the company. For some unknown reason, the boss's son made me leave the office within one or two days of notice without prior conversation with his father. Everyone was in shock. I was totally petrified by the sudden notice. They paid me a chunk slice of money to leave the company and off I went.

My mother saw me in such devastation that she suggested I go to the USA to see my best friend, Noriko, and my God-sister, Judy, for a few days. In just under two weeks I had my air ticket booked for the US. I had originally planned this trip to be eight days, but it turned into six weeks! It was one of the best things I have done in my whole entire life. I enjoyed so much of the travelling within the six weeks of time!

Bear in mind my mother has always been an extremely thrifty person. However, she could see that I really needed to get out of the scene at that point in time. In a critical time like this, my mother's supportive words have given me great guidance. I ended up having a great time in the US and Canada, spent a lot of time with my best friend, and had a great tour around the US and Canada, visiting all the museums, universities, and dining out with my friends. It was indeed a sensational time over in both the US and Canada. It broadened my spectrum in life.

After I returned back from the beautiful trip, I was able to find another job within four weeks' time. I was ready to start all over again, nice and refreshed, ready to rock with the jungle again.

My mother's unconditional love had taught me that it is OK to stumble in life. Her words will always be there, her hugs will always be warm, and her doors will always be open.

It was the support that has established the foundation of trust again, the belief of an "I can do it" spirit, the strength built in your inner self to be strong. The love that needs to be reinforced. Once the inner strength had been built based on love, on the unconditional love from my mother, I knew I had grown stronger. This strength cannot be taken away externally, because it has been firmly substantiated inside.

Interestingly enough, life always presented itself with different formats to try love. Only unconditional love can pass through all these trials; because people love you unconditionally, they do not expect you in return, but only hope for your wellbeing. That is how my parents' love is to me. The only way I pay them back is to show them my independence and well being. That is the best reward they want from me.

CHAPTER 15

Finding Yourself, Who You Really Are

The unexamined life is not worth living.
~Socrates

When I finally re-established trust in myself, it was time to go. It was time to spread my wings and fly, fly off from my parents.

After I had been back in Taiwan for twelve years, I realized that I really did not like it there. It is quite ambiguous. I was stuck. I did not like my lifestyle there, but the twelve years of reconciliation really helped me to step up to another level psychologically. Twelve years of staying with my parents had filled the eight years of empty hollowness without family around. I was sort of stuck in a comfort zone myself that I was not ready to get out of. The twelve years had fulfilled their primary purpose on a complimentary level. I found what was lost, and I found what needed to be re-acknowledged—the love from my parents. I needed both of my parents' presences to ensure I was well loved.

On the other hand, I knew something was not right. Being back in Taiwan was mainly to be with my parents, but what about my personal life, my love life, my personal growth? Well, when you have been abandoned or left alone in a foreign country for so long, you become accustomed to being alone. I became quite self-reliant. I spent a lot of time alone thinking. I needed a lot of space alone. I often wondered what I wanted next in life, instead of cruising along with the rest of the world. I am a strong believer of individualism. Everyone is unique. It is not typical for me to be conventional. Life has given me a very different experience, hence my perspective of things has become quite different. Thinking makes me examine my life constantly.

It takes a lot of effort to get out of your comfort zone. When there is a life card calling, then you know it is time to move on.

Sometimes the calling card present its way in a vicious format. In my last two years of staying in Taiwan, I worked in a dental supply company. I felt quite neutral towards my job, neither like it or hate it; it just paid the bills, and it was just a job. After I had been with the company for three months, there were changes in the higher ranks of the company. Our former General Manager had been replaced by another one, and political issues were quite tense. The new GM did not like me simply because he did not see my enthusiasm. I was just simply doing what I was doing. I was reluctant to kiss someone's ass at that point in time. I was disgusted.

In the administrative role as I was working, the most difficult hurdle presented was the lack of knowledge that people had in the licensing part of medical devices. There were so many accreditation documents and trivial points to look at. This new GM wanted to have his sales and he would do anything to achieve that, and sometimes the way he did it could be quite harsh and direct.

A couple of months after he was on board, there was a lack of communication. He could sense that I had no intention to expand what I was doing, and he was very unhappy with my performance. One day, he told me—"You are OVERPAID!" That statement really struck me.

I was extremely pissed off. Even if it was the truth, it is quite offensive to have said this to somebody. It is just telling people that you are not worthwhile, and you are incompetent. That was when I eventually made the decision to leave Taiwan. I knew that if I was considering looking for other job opportunities, I would be encountering similar situations. My mind was simply not present while I was working. I needed something different. I needed to find out who I really was. I needed to head back to Australia, to Sydney to pick up things where I left off fifteen years ago when I left in a hurry with my mother.

I left Sydney with my mother in a hurry after eight years of living there. At that point in time, I was quite sick mentally, hence things were not working out. We packed twenty-three boxes in the basement and I never returned to that property for fifteen years. We quickly packed everything and scurried off.

Fifteen years later I had the chance to come back to Sydney and checked out my property again. When I saw the boxes lying in the basement of the house, I went completely crashed. I cried as much as I could when I went off. It was very emotional. Later on I packed everything away and got rid of all the old stuff. There were things that you will always remember, the things you write in teenage years that do not make sense. The overwhelming sensation lasted for days before I could come back to my senses.

After I come back to Sydney, I visited every single place I missed over the years. My old school, the street I used to live on, the places I used to hang out with friends, my old mate's place, and even my ex's former residence. When I finally reached the opera house and Harbour Bridge, I was in tears. I told myself, *I am finally here. Twelve years I have been away. AND I am here NOW.*

I went back to Sydney University, the very building where I'd had my hand injury. I stepped slowly and carefully in the process contemplating things in the past. I was quite emotional in the process, but I took my time. I went all by myself; I did not want any company. I knew I had to face the memories all over again, and to say a proper goodbye to them. Unfortunately it is a pathway you can go by yourself, to say a proper goodbye.

Once I said goodbye, I accepted the fact that those was just parts of my life, pieces of me. It is impossible to forget the whole thing, but I have come to recognize that this is part of the learning curve. The most important lesson I've learned in life is that you have to be honest to yourself. At the end of the day you can probably fool anyone else, but not yourself.

It was a great choice to come back and pick up things where I'd left off years ago. It compliments all the feelings of loss I have had over the years. However the process was quite emotional. It is hard to come back to the point where you left off and say a proper GOODBYE. Goodbye to the old memories, goodbye to the lessons that life has given me, and THANK YOU. Then I was able to step up to the next level and carry on with life. It is part of the process, a life review. To have a proper way to close one chapter of my life. To also appreciate the life lessons given to me. It is ALL good.

CHAPTER 16

Re-Establish Where You Left Off Fifteen Years Ago

I just felt that you can't have a character fall in love so madly
as they did in the last movie and not finish it off, understand it,
get some closure. That's why the movie is called
'Quantum of Solace'—that's exactly what he's looking for.
-Daniel Craig

Once you close a chapter of your life properly, then you can move forward with the next one.

I did not like my life back in Taiwan for twelve years. I felt quite foreign in terms of my mentality. Despite the fact that I have fulfilled the gap of love between my parents and myself, things were not quite right. I then decided to come back to Sydney. Before I came back to Sydney, I needed a total two years of preparation. It was quite hard.

When you finally overcome the mental fear, then the reality kicks in. It is hard both emotionally and financially. I had to start things all from scratch—well, almost. I had to pick up my language skills, which was difficult for a few reasons. First of all, English is not my first language. Secondly, I had never been working in Sydney before. It was a whole lot of challenges to me. I had to re-learn the workforce structure, had to learn the language used at work, and had to learn the right terminology for it. Things were not easy, and I needed to take one step at a time. Regardless of whether I was a fast learner or not, things still needed some time.

When I first came back I refused to see all the old schoolmates from high school, partly because they reminded me of the sad old memories. It was not their fault; I simply associated them with the old sad memories. I needed to start all over again.

I stayed with a Jewish lady. I wanted to re-establish my life and being an Aussie! That was a mistake and misconception. The fact is, I will never, and can never, deny the fact that I am an Asian. On the other hand, I did not want to face them my old friends because most of them were quite established already. I do not want to be in the category to be compared. I needed some time alone.

The lady I stayed with really looked after me well. She had taken me under her wings when I first came back. Without her support, I think things would be quite different. It was a time of self-confrontation, and the six months away from the workforce gave me ample time of solitude. It was great. Unfortunately things did not end on good terms between me and her. I think that I was always looking for a mother figure. And she told me that she was not my mother, since the mental pressure I put on her was so paramount that she could not handle it at some point. Perhaps it would be easier if our relationship were based on landlord and tenant.

It is an interesting point. People are conditioned to certain things; there are certain ways people behave. I remember reading a psychological report stating that victims of abusive childhoods will always look for an abusive relationship in their adulthood, simply because they feel it is safe. It could possibly expand to their relationships with their boss, their relationships with future partners, etc. I personally know a friend who behaves like this. She was physically abused at a young age and she grew up to constantly find someone who abused her—either it would be her superior or in a relationship.

The opposite was true for me. As the result of lack of parental love in my teenage years, I always find people to compensate for the feeling of loss.

If I find a good mother figure, I will attach my yearning for love to this motherly figure. I got confused with the role playing. It was a way to attract attention. I am simply an attention-seeker. I need people to notice me. It happened between the landlady and me, too. She treated me very well initially, like her own daughter. Over time I became quite clingy to the point that she could not cope. Eventually things came to the end, and it was time to move out. She had a perfect point: she is not my mother. It is easier to maintain a businesslike relationship. It is unfair to have her attached to my personal emotions.

Along the way, people will always associate things with familiarity. Creating identification is the hardest thing to start with, but making rectifications or changes to it are also huge steps. It always takes two to tangle. When things go wrong, I learned to stop for a second. Before starting the process of finger pointing, I would think about the part I had played, and think about which section did not go right because of ME.

Being honest is always the primary key to face life. Being honest to yourself is crucial. If one cannot be totally honest about themselves then they are limiting their potential for improvement. In the years of solitude, I learned this the hard way. Now I have come to appreciate it.

Looking for a job in Sydney was a nightmare. The Australians are very conservative people. The main prerequisite to find a job locally was to have "local experience". This is a catch-twenty-two; if you do not have local experience to start with, how and where do you start? One has to start from somewhere, right?

It took me more than three years to re-establish myself in Sydney. Looking back, I am appreciative that I have come through all those hard times.

CHAPTER 17

Graduation—We Are Proud of You

A graduation ceremony is an event where the commencement
speaker tells thousands of students dressed in identical caps
and gowns that 'individuality' is the key to success.
~Robert Orben

I did not finish my bachelor's degree in Sydney (I went to Sydney University). I could not finish my degree as a result of both physical and mental fatigue. Years of distress have caused my inability to present my own self.

It was an unfinished business that eventually needed to be dealt with.

Over the years back in Taiwan, I always thought of finishing my degree and/or coming back to Sydney when I retired. I had given thought to doing both by the time I was in my sixties. I am grateful that I have accomplished this a lot earlier.

I have always loved psychology and the study of human mind. It is intriguing. It fascinates me. When I first attempted my bachelor's as a pharmacy degree, I did not like it. The chemistry and biochemistry really gave me hard time. I had no idea what all those atoms and the equations were about. My brain was just not set for it. Luckily I never needed it after those years! Tell me whoever had to pick up the periodic table after studying years?

Perhaps if I did not have all those mind-boggling matters, I would be able to get my degree without loathing it. However my mind was not present. It was too hard for me. Instead, I really loved reading people's minds. I love seeing people's reactions towards things. Guess what? My matriarchal mother had threatened me that she would not support me if I studied psychology. She thinks people doing psychology degree would get crazy? A pharmacy degree and practice as a pharmacist simply meant solid working money. Yes, again, I needed to obey the rule. THE MONEY RULE. You do as you are told, or else . . . .

Yes, more unfinished business, not being able to finish my degree in due course, has served more resentment.

Eventually I decided to come back to Sydney. The only way to convince my mother of the necessity of my move was that I needed to finish a degree, any degree of some sort. It actually sounds stupid that I needed to get my mother's consent to do this. Yes, it is stupid.

One day I was browsing online and I actually found an online course that is made available from Sydney University, yes, the one where I could not complete my original degree. Sydney University offers online courses for master's degrees! I was quite ecstatic to learn this. Julia had a chance!

Well, I needed a bachelor's before I could apply for a master's degree, right? I found a college that could offer both night classes and prerequisite classes for students preparing to go overseas to study. I was on my way to finishing my bachelor's degree and applying for a master's degree with the University of Sydney later. I took as many units I could to fulfil the competence to finish the bachelor's degree within fifteen months—provided they waived the units I have had from Sydney University previously.

Over the fifteen months' time, I was working during the day and went to classes at night, including weekends. During weekdays, I usually came back by 10:30 pm. It was quite exhausting but fulfilling. I picked up my books again and studied. It was actually quite a different sensation as a mature student; I actually enjoyed the course. I filled myself with laughter. I knew I was one step closer to leaving Taiwan for Sydney. It is the pathway that I had always yearned for.

Incidentally, I finally had the chance to do some social science studies—psychology was my favourite!

When I finally finished my bachelor's degree, it took me no time to apply for the postgraduate degree available. The course I applied for was Intellectual Disability, the study of people who are handicapped. I had very limited knowledge of what I was heading into, but it looked quite interesting to me. I applied for the July intake, but the university only took this course for February intake for the following year. So they accepted me to do two core subjects in the second semester so I could complete the units earlier to accumulate credits without delay. In August of 2009, I was on my way back to Sydney. I finally went back!

When I got my study materials I had no idea what I was reading. I have never been exposed to intellectual people or kids. My initial essay was poorly done, not only was the English very badly written but also the contents were disastrous. One additional problem was that I need to go and observe some handicapped children as part of my study. The lady I stayed with tried to hook me up with her associates to the special institutes to be with those kids. Unfortunately they never replied to my request or e-mail. Time had lapsed and it was approaching the assignment's due date. I did not know what to do . . . .

One day as I passed by the Tzu Chi Buddhist Foundation, I happened to come across an old friend. He told me that the Tzu Chi used to sponsor a special school near the Dural area. He took out the map and tried to show me where it was, but he could not come up with its name. Now, that was a big challenge!

The next day my landlady was kind enough to offer me her car and I took the chances to find out where this school was located. The morning I left, I had told myself that I would not come home without having something substantial with me!

As I was driving around the Dural area, I actually got quite lost. I tried to ring my old friend up to see if he could indicate a right pathway, but it did not seem to work. I was driving in circles. So I decided to stop over by the road and see if I could find any neighbours who knew the area. Magically after I stepped out of the car, I heard dogs barking. I saw this old lady watering her garden, so I asked her, "Excuse me, do you know if there is any special school around?"

"Yes," she answered me. "It is at the back of this street."

I followed her instructions and found the school. Interestingly the school has a very intriguing gate. It was sort of half open. I opened the gate, feeling like a thief or intruder, and then I was in! By this time my adventurous spirit had gotten a bit overwhelmed and I needed a toilet break. I entered the very first building I saw, and there was a toilet there. I thought, okay, let's do this first and we will worry about other things later.

After alleviating the usual pressure from toileting, my adventure continued. There was this long corridor that I had gone past, and eventually I found a big room with the door half opened. I knocked and went into the room and tried my luck.

"Excuse me, I am a student of the Sydney University for Intellectual Disability Studies. I am looking into possibly observing special kids so I could work on a report. I am also from the Tzu-Chi Buddhist Foundation. This is how I got to know of your school." As I was talking to her, I showed her my study book and my identification of the Tzu Chi Buddhist Foundation.

This lady took off her reading glasses and stared at me. She must have been quite astonished to see this Asian intruder coming into her door! After she had seen the proof of my study and badges from the Tzu Chi Buddhist Foundation, she felt secure that I was a genuine student simply looking for places to practice her study.

It turned out that she was the principal of the school! Soon after that she then referred me to one of the classes for observation. Two weeks later I was in the class for observation. My academic results progressed well, improving bit by bit. The result turned out to be quite good towards the end of the semester. Of course, I had some help from my friend.

One day during November that year (2009), I got a phone call from the university. The course coordinator called to let me know that "intellectual disability" would no longer running in the year of 2010. I needed to apply for other courses. It was quite unfair, but sometimes things are meant to be.

The semester after that I tried to apply other online courses available, but they were all denied. I decided to go back to the university to see if they could do anything for me. I said to the course coordinator, "I have come a long way to come back to Sydney to finish a master's degree, but this is not what you are allowing me to do." I almost cried.

Unfortunately there was not much they could do. Whilst I was talking to the course coordinator, I saw this course brochure, "Master's of Sexual Health." It was offered online! As a mature student, I could not afford to be a full-time student; I needed to work during the day to support myself. Online study was a perfect option for this!

"Is this course going to go for a while?" I asked the course coordinator.

"Yes, it is".

So that was it. I applied to this course and I got accepted! Then I was on my way to finish this one! When I first applied for it, I only got accepted as a graduate certificate, (graduate certificate requires twenty-four credit points; graduate diploma requires thirty-six credit points, and a master's degree requires forty-eight credit points). They were kind enough to waive the previous twelve credit points I had done for intellectual disability studies, which means I only needed another one semester of twelve credit points to finish off my graduate certificate!

I have to be honest and admit that I was only doing this course for the sake of vanity to fulfil the unfinished business of my bachelor's degree when in my early twenties. At this point in time I had already gotten an administrative role working in a pharmaceutical company. I really did not think I needed another degree for my job.

However, I went to see the course professor towards the end of the semester to see if this course could offer me some sort of job prospect. We had an hour of chat and the professor was quite intrigued by my experience of getting into this course. She talked me into completing a master's degree. *A master's degree*, I said to myself. Julia, you are going to get a master's degree! That day I went home feeling quite sentimental. Fifteen years ago I was struggling to finish a bachelor's degree, and here I was—on my way to finishing a master's degree! Woo la la!

Believe me, the course itself was very intriguing. As time went by, my English was picking up. I was improving.

One morning in November of 2010, I woke up and applied some essence oil on myself, trying to relieve some daily pressure. Incidentally the drops went into my eyes. My right eye had gone quite swollen. I went straight to the emergency room and luckily I did not have to wait for long. In thirty minutes I had been attended to by the doctors. They used lots of distilled water to rinse the essence oil out of my eyes. The process took approximately thirty to forty minutes to eventually rinse all of the residue out of my eyes. At the end the process, the doctor had to cover my right eye. There were really friendly doctors. They could see me suffering. "Hello, pirate eye" the doctor greeted me. Sometimes things just get a bit easier with a sense of humour!

I went home with vision in only one eye. On top of that, I felt quite sick. I had the flu and a running stomach! It was a Thursday that I injured myself. I had to turn into a paper the next Monday—online, of course. To go through the special consideration process with the university (a process that allows you to postpone handing in your assignment), actually takes longer. It would just be easier for me to finish the work over the weekend and hand it in! So there I was, working so hard over the weekend with only one functioning eye. It turned out that I got an 85% for that very assignment! I was quite pleased with myself!

I had eventually finished my degree by the end of 2011. It was a sensational process. I absolutely enjoyed my course.

My parents came over for my graduation in March of 2012. The pair of them were absolutely ecstatic when they attended the ceremony. I never really knew if they exactly knew the nature of my course. Every time they asked me, I mentioned it lightly. When I got my graduation certificate, I was sort of afraid either one of them would scrutinize word-by-word. Well, the words "sex," or "sexual health" could be quite compelling, even though my parents had limited English, but the word "sex" could also be quite distinctive, too.

I have successfully completed this course to finish a master's degree. What I am going to do with it will eventually unfold with life. Perhaps there is a sequel for this book? Who knows? Let's wait and see.

CHAPTER 18
Love Stories

Sometimes the heart sees what is invisible to the eye.
~H. Jackson Brown, Jr.

Gathering insightful stories became one of my hobbies, too. I love seeing beauty in people, and the love they present in many different forms. It is sensational.

The Couple I Met in Canada

I had an absolutely sensational trip in both the US and Canada for six weeks. Every morning I woke up with joy. This is the couple I met on my Canada trip.

When I was in Vancouver I took the bus to visit the city. The bus was run by wire-route. I was in the front of the bus by the driver, waiting to take off. All of the sudden the driver had to make a sudden stop. Due to inertia, everyone moved forward as the result of the sudden stop.

There was this old lady beside me so I was trying to hold onto her to make sure she was okay and not falling. After everything was settled, she looked at me with a sparkling eye, telling me she was okay with a gesture of appreciation.

She said to me, "It is my sixtieth anniversary next Thursday."

Before I had anything to say back, the man behind her said, "And I am still in love with her." I stared at her again—she had the most beautiful smile on earth I have ever seen on her wrinkled face.

My Mother's Definition of Love (Comic Version)

My mother has a problem understanding foreign soap operas or films. Even with subtitles she finds it hard to understand what has been portrayed in the story. When she was living in Sydney with me, someone told her it would be good to watch soap operas on a daily basis to improve her level of English. So she did. She is a good student, as she has always been. There is this American soap that has been on forever called "The Bold and the Beautiful." She watched it every day religiously right in front of the TV.

One day, she came to me and told me that the two main characters loved each other! I was quite astonished to learn my mother had finally gotten the language!

My mother said, "He loves her!"

I asked her, "How did you know they love each other?"

She replied "He kissed her!"

Sometimes it does not take too much to illustrate what has to be said. Only a simple action will do.

My Parents' Love to Each Other

My mother's unconditional love also applies to my dearest father. Due to the onset of my father's health condition, his inability to function properly at times has caused tension to the family both financially and emotionally. My mother managed to keep everything under control by holding tightly to the finances at home.

I remember when I was five, I saw my parents hugging each other. My father apologetically said to my mother, "I am sorry, I don't want to be like this either." They were both buried in tears whilst hugging. As a five-year-old, this image had such a strong impact. It also gave me the definition of unconditional love between husband and wife. Love is not only about holding onto each other at good times, but most importantly during very harsh periods. My parents set good examples of this.

The pair of them hardly ever fought over the years of marriage. They managed to hold hands during the harsh periods. My mother always taught me that if my father raised his voice, she would keep her mouth shut until my father came over and apologized. He usually comes back patiently. If my mother raised her voice, my father would immediately know that he was in trouble and that he needed to shut up.

Their relationship was completely complimentary to each other. If either of them found out things were not going right, they would hold on to their breath and eventually the pair of them come to agreement. They did not raise voices during conflicts, which is an excellent example to learn from. It is important to remain calm and collected at all times, because you never know when life will come to you with different forms of challenges.

Despite my father's health condition, he is actually a jolly person. He loves smiling. Sometimes I consider him as a jolly monkey who has a lot of cheekiness in him.

When my father was going through some high emotions, he could really pick on my mother badly. He would use harsh abusive words to embarrass my mother, sometimes even in public! My mother always seemed to tolerate it and was able to put up with it. She never took it seriously. She sometimes shouted back, forgetting my father was actually a patient, and that he was not being himself at the time. Moments later when he came back to his senses, he would go repent to my mother. If I could turn those moments into life, they really sound quite funny,. Love is about compromise, and I see that within my parents' love to each other.

It is perhaps worthwhile mentioning the longest time my parents fought with each other when they were younger. It happened with

I was approximately ten years old. It lasted approximately less than forty-eight hours. The pair of them fought over things that they did not agree with. My father got on his high horse and kept scolding on my mother for hours without stopping. Usually their fights would take less than three hours or so, but this one broke the record. It was so severe they would not talk to each other.

The next day after the fight, my mother seemed quite upset and was ready to go back to her countryside house due to my father's irrational behaviour. My mother was in tears sending both my brother and myself off to school and asked us to behave. Because it was quite new that my parents would fight for so long, and my mother had always been the domineering figure at home, we childishly thought it was actually nice and fresh to have my mother away for a few days. To our surprise, they reconciled the day we came home from school happily.

Later on my mother told me the unfolding story of that morning. She had the household sorted and was ready to go back to her country house that morning. She had gone out of the door and realized that she forgot her bank book at home, so she returned back to the house and got it from the drawer. My father was still in the house with anger. He shouted at my mother fumingly, "You kneel down!" My mother did as what she was told; she knelt down. After that, the scene contained a bit of personal intimacy that I am not supposed to divulge. Guess what? They reconciled within seconds after that. "Love is all about compromise," my mother said. Things will eventually work themselves out. With love, you will always need faith.

Magpie Story

This would be a perfect way to depict separation anxiety.

After I came back to Sydney I was still struggling to grow out of my mother, emotionally. Finances thereafter were tight with the emotional string. I was crying my head off not knowing what to do. My friend and I sat in the park talking about it, and saw this scene . . . .

This mother magpie was trying to push the baby magpie away to grow independently. (Mother Magpie has whole black-coloured feathers and the baby magpies have gray-coloured feathers).

After the mother magpie had fed the baby Magpie, she wanted to push the little one to grow independently. The mother Magpie urged her baby aside fiercely, pretending to be cruel. After the baby Magpie had gone a bit further, the mother secretly followed her baby behind to see if she was alright without the baby noticing.

"Perhaps this is what your mother should do," said my friend. "She should allow you to grow out of her. She should learn."

My mother always wants to protect me in her own way, to patronize me. She so wishes that she could collect me when I fall. But she has to learn to let me fall and that I can stand back on my own feet. I have my own life to live. She cannot always be there. It is a lesson we both need to learn, to live independently from each other emotionally, co-existing. Every time I encountered problems and went home to her with tears, she would always be there to comfort me. She would be there to offer her suggestions. It is her very way to show that she loves me. Sometimes I think it might even be good for me to fall! Perhaps I need to learn things in the hard way?! And then I will be able to stand back on my own terms. I need to grow out from her emotionally, at the same time telling her I will be just fine, as it has been and it will always be: FINE.

CHAPTER 19
My Words to My Mother

A loving heart is the beginning of all knowledge.
~Thomas Carlyle

When I was younger, I always resented having gone through the dark eight years living in Sydney filled with sorrow. It was a lonely journey to have to confront a lot of dark hours by myself at young age. At some point I felt like I was the only person left in this world.

It feels like I was an infant bird who had not been taught to fly properly, but was being pushed out of the cliff. Maybe there were dangers at the back end and the best approach was to push the little birds off the cliff? One has to take chances, right? The infant bird has to learn how to spread her wings on her own terms. Over the period of time, she stumbles, flies off the rocks and eventually finds her way back to align herself. It might take a bit longer to come back to her senses, but eventually she does. She learns things the hard way, but everything turns out to be OK.

Miraculously with luck, in desperate times when I cried out for help there were always people helping me. I was like a drowning person who incidentally found some kind of log to hold onto. When there is the log, you hold onto it until a bigger boat or ship comes to collect you. The important key is to have faith. To believe that every lesson holds its own meanings, hence it will equip you with strength.

Although leaving me behind was not the best thing to do, my mother figured it was the BEST option she could come up with. It was a hard choice, one that has kept me resentful over the years until I found the balance point.

Now when I think back I learn how to appreciate things. The hardest thing is to appreciate hurdles and the lessons I have learned from them. The strength I have developed over the years is amazing. It is like I have collected enough tools in my box and could easily access to them when the time comes.

Trust me, it is hard to face yourself with absolute honesty. It might be easier just to blame someone else until the core problem comes back and bites you, and it bites you hard! I also learned how to look at things from a very different angle. There are things I learned from years of isolation and independence which trained me to confront the hurdles of work and life. I continued to learn and grow. Sometimes in life you just need that push to move ahead, otherwise you will always be stuck in your comfort zone. Living in a comfort zone is not exactly a bad thing, but you will later on regret or wonder, "what if?" What if I did this, what if I did that . . . what if . . . . ? But things will never come into fruition with "what if." Like the NIKE spirit, JUST DO IT.

On the other hand, life might come to you as a real push to get you out of your comfort zone. You never know. Life is unexpected.

Stepping out of your comfort zone is like going for a swim: the initial jump could be hard and fearful, but once you get into the water and get accustomed to the water temperature, things become easier.

There are things that happened that you may not know why and how at the time. Later on in life answers float above water to present themselves, and that is when you say, *Ah-ha*. All of a sudden things start to click. All the mist at the front has disappeared.

There are so many things I have learned throughout the journey. I have been able to carry on based on the foundation of my mother's unconditional love.

Mommy, I love you—with all my heart.

www.alovenotetomytigermom.com